The Book of Sports Lists

Who among us ... ...ds of lists. Shopping ... ...sts, guest lists, lists of chores.

So many of us are compulsive list-makers. It's seductive. We make lists of favorite foods, favorite songs, favorite movies. Some of us even make lists of lists.

Sports is especially conducive to list-making, and there isn't anyone—fan or athlete—who has not gotten into the game of lists. We choose the best and the worst, the biggest and the smallest, the strongest and the weakest, the wildest and the weirdest.

With this in mind, the editors polled hundreds of celebrities in and out of sports: writers, broadcasters, and an assortment of others with a penchant for making lists. This book is the result of that poll.

The attributed lists are authentic. Others are the brainchildren of the editors. We thank those who responded to our request for lists and we apologize to those whose lists did not make our list of lists.

We hope there will be a second *Book of Sports Lists,* and we invite you, the reader, to participate. Send your list to:

Associated Features
370 Lexington Avenue
New York, NY 10017

Do it today. Don't delay. Put it at the top of your list!

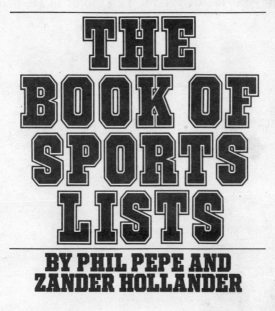

THE BOOK OF SPORTS LISTS

BY PHIL PEPE AND ZANDER HOLLANDER

An Associated Features Book

PINNACLE BOOKS   LOS ANGELES

6 of the Most Outstanding Young People in the World, to Whom This Book Is Dedicated

1. Susan Hollander
2. Peter Hollander
3. Jayne Pepe
4. David Pepe
5. Jimmy Pepe
6. John Carl Pepe

EDITOR'S NOTE: This list is chronological and not necessarily in order of preference.

THE BOOK OF SPORTS LISTS

Copyright © 1979 by Associated Features Inc.

An original Pinnacle Books edition, published for the first time anywhere.

First printing, June 1979

ISBN: 0-523-40472-7

Cover illustration by Bob Cassell

Printed in the United States of America

PINNACLE BOOKS, INC.
2029 Century Park East
Los Angeles, California 90067

Contents

VII THE BODY BEAUTIFUL   *161*

VIII WHEELS   *175*

IX MAKING LOVE, IN THE ROUGH   *191*

X   WINTER GAMES   *209*

XI   BY A NOSE   *229*

I

That's Entertainment

Ronald Reagan's 6 Greatest
Sports Movies

1. "Knute Rockne—All-American"
2. "The Winning Team"
3. "Pride of the Yankees"
4. "The Stratton Story"
5. "Brian's Song"
6. "Little Mo"

Says Mr. Reagan: "It's only coincidence that I played George 'Gipper' Gipp in one ('Knute Rockne—All-American') and Old Alex (Grover Cleveland Alexander) himself in the other ('The Winning Team')."

Mr. Reagan also recounts his favorite story as a football broadcaster:

"Back in my sportscasting days, a new program director, and therefore my boss, decided he wanted to get in on the Saturday afternoon games. He arranged to do this by teaming himself with me to do the pre-game and between-half color.

Ronald Reagan as the Gipper of Notre Dame in "Knute Rockne—All American." *UPI*

"Our first team effort was an Iowa-Nebraska game in the U. of Iowa stadium. With two minutes of the first half remaining, Nebraska was out in front, 14-0. Then Iowa's sophomore—a lad named Ozzie Simmons, who would become nationally known—broke loose, scoring two touchdowns in those two minutes. The half ended, 14-14, and my new teammate was as wild as the crowd in the stadium.

"He grabbed the mike as the gun sounded and told our radio audience: 'Ladies and gentlemen, down here in the purple haze of an Indian summer afternoon, lightning has just struck twice with the rapidity of a serpent.' "

As a baseball broadcaster, Mr. Reagan did the Chicago Cubs' games for a station in Des Moines, Iowa. The following is his favorite baseball story:

"I don't think a single incident in any of the games I broadcast as a sports announcer impressed me so much as the last few weeks of the 1935 National League season. The Cubs came to a point where their only mathematical chance for winning the pennant lay in winding up the season, 21 games in all, without a defeat.

"As the totals started to mount, and they reached 15, then 16, without a defeat, you just couldn't believe it would happen. They went on and finished the season winning the last 21 games without a break. This, I believe, certainly was the biggest and most sustained thrill I ever had in broadcasting."

Rex Reed's 10 Best Sports Movies Ever Made

1. "The Stratton Story"
2. "Visions of Eight"
3. "Pride of the Yankees"
4. "Pat and Mike"
5. "Fat City"
6. "Bang the Drum Slowly"
7. "Requiem for a Heavyweight"
8. "Champion"
9. "Downhill Racer"
10. "The Hustler"

Rex Reed's 10 Worst Sports Movies Ever Made

1. "Take Me Out to the Ballgame"
2. "Jim Thorpe—All-American"
3. "One on One"
4. "Slap Shot"
5. "The Babe Ruth Story"
6. "The Endless Summer"
7. "Golden Boy"
8. "Knute Rockne—All-American"
9. "Angels in the Outfield"
10. "The Great American Pastime"

Jimmy Stewart and June Allyson in "The Stratton Story."

MGM

Anthony Quinn and Julie Harris in "Requiem for a Heavyweight."

Columbia

Jerry Della Femina's 11 Greatest Advertising Campaigns Using Sports Personalities

Jerry Della Femina is chairman of the board of Della Femina, Travisano & Partners, Inc., one of the most creative advertising agencies. He was named "Advertising Executive of the Year" in 1970. He is also the author of the best-selling book on advertising, "From Those Wonderful Folks Who Gave Us Pearl Harbor."

1. Miller's Lite Beer is perhaps the best known and most effective campaign using sports heroes in advertising history.
2. Camel cigarettes for years showed how Camels were mild for Joe DiMaggio's T-zone.
3. Joe DiMaggio for Mr. Coffee. The only reason this was

George Steinbrenner and Billy Martin in their classic TV commercial for Lite Beer from Miller. *Lite Beer from Miller/McCann-Erickson*

Joe DiMaggio bats clean-up for Mr. Coffee. *Mr. Coffee/Ted Bates & Co.*

successful was because of DiMaggio's husky voice, which he developed from smoking Camels.

4. Bristol-Myers for Vitalis with Muhammad Ali and Joe Frazier. They were able to fund this commercial by offering Ali and Frazier a piece of any additional profits. There were no additional profits, apparently, and both Ali and Frazier took a beating.

5. Ozon Hairspray was the first commercial where heavy, masculine baseball players (Hank Bauer, Yogi Berra, and Joe Pepitone) admitted they were sissies for using their wives' hairspray. These commercials obviously made a very strong impression on a young kid named Dave Kopay, who wanted to be a football player. He decided not to use his wife's hairspray, but to become a sissy.

6. Sam Snead for Bromo-Seltzer, where he said, "On the day of atonement, I cannot afford to be sick." Years later, the Jewish part of the audience realized that Sammy was not referring to Yom Kippur, but could not pronounce "tournament" like other white folk.

7. Rocky Graziano selling Breakstone as the cultured yogurt.

8. Bill Russell sinking a shot in his office after delivering a great commercial for the telephone company.

9. Wilt Chamberlain for Volkswagen cars. Unfortunately, the seats were so tight and Chamberlain's legs were so long that he appeared to be performing an obscene act on himself.

10. All of the early Gillette baseball spots featuring such names as Billy Southworth, Joe McCarthy, Leo Durocher, etc., talking about having shaved the morning of the game with Gillette Blue Blades.

11. Joe Namath selling popcorn machines, pantyhose, toasters, personnel agencies, movies, Johnnie Walker Black, Brut, and, most of all, Joe Namath.

Della Femina adds: "Of the list, Joe Namath is probably the man who has performed in the worst commercials of any athlete."

Ernie Harwell's 12 Greatest
Sports Songs

Ernie Harwell is the veteran baseball broadcaster for the Detroit Tigers, and a songwriter. He has written many songs, including "Move Over Babe, Here Comes Henry," and his tunes have been recorded by B.J. Thomas, Homer & Jethro, Merilee Rush, Barbara Lewis, Betty Lavette, Deon Jackson, and others.

1. "Take Me Out to the Ball Game," the classic sports song that has outlasted all of them
2. "Mr. Touchdown, U.S.A.," saluting every American male's fantasy
3. "You've Got To Be a Football Hero," again the gridiron dream
4. "Notre Dame Victory March," the one that makes all the other school marches provincial
5. "Straight Down the Middle," Bing Crosby's salute to golf
6. "Fugue for Tin Horns," the Sinatra number from "Guys and Dolls"
7. "The Game," comedy and insight from "Damn Yankees"
8. "Van Lingle Mungo," nostalgic names from the jazz performer, Dave Frishberg
9. "Joltin' Joe DiMaggio," Les Brown's tribute to DiMag's streak
10. "We Are The Champions," a spirited modern tune by Queen
11. "Beetlebaum," the comic racing tale by Spike Jones
12. "Move Over Babe, Here Comes Henry"—this one makes it because Ernie Harwell, co-writer with Bill Slayback, compiled the list

Jonathan Schwartz' 8 Greatest Sports Songs

Jonathan Schwartz, a deejay on New York's WNEW, confesses that two of the great loves of his life are music and baseball. His legion of fans will attest that he is knowledgeable in both.

1. "Take Me Out to the Ball Game," a marvelously constructed song
2. "Notre Dame Victory March"
3. "I'm a Rambling Wreck From Georgia Tech"
4. "Van Lingle Mungo," by Dave Frishberg
5. "There Used To Be a Ballpark Here," not truly a sports song, but a beautiful work by a great songwriter, Joe Reposo
6. "Fugue for Tin Horns," from "Guys and Dolls"
7. "I Could Pass That Football," from "Wonderful Town," written by Betty Comden and Adolph Green, and Leonard Bernstein
8. "And the Red Sox Are Winning," by Earth Opera, 1967

Thurman Munson's 10 Favorite Sportswriters

The New York Yankees' captain and catcher recently co-authored his autobiography for Coward McCann, & Geoghegan. The title of the book was NOT "How To Win Friends and Influence People."

1.
2.
3.
4.
5.

6.
7.
8.
9.
10.

John Leonard's All-Time List of Sports Reading Matter

John Leonard, formerly book editor of the *New York Times,* now writes a general column for that newspaper. His list, he says, is in no particular order, but is broken down by category.

JOGGING

1. "The Loneliness of the Long Distance Runner," by Alan Sillitoe

GAMBLING

1. "The Gambler," by Dostoyevsky

HUNTING AND FISHING

1. "A Sportsman's Sketches," by Ivan Turgenev
2. "The Old Man and the Sea," by Ernest Hemingway
3. "The Warren Commission Report on the Assasination of John F. Kennedy"
4. "Moby Dick," by Herman Melville

BASEBALL

1. "The Universal Baseball Association," by Robert Coover
2. "The Natural," by Bernard Malamud
3. "The Great American Novel," by Philip Roth
4. Anything by Roger Angell
5. The wrapper on a Reggie Bar

CHESS

1. Anything by Vladimir Nabokov

OTHER INDOOR SPORTS

1. The Kinsey and Hite Reports
2. "The Story of O"
3. Anything by Norman Mailer

FOOTBALL

1. "End Zone," by Don DeLillo
2. "A Fan's Notes," by Fred Exley

HORSES

1. Any biography of Catherine the Great

BASKETBALL

1. "Rabbit Run," by John Updike
2. "Drive, He Said," by Jeremy Larner
3. John McPhee on Bill Bradley

RABBITS

1. "Watership Down," by Richard Adams

BIRDS

1. Audubon

BUTTERFLIES

1. Also anything by Nabokov

CRIME

1. "The Book of Job"
2. "Crime and Punishment," by Dostoyevsky

HOCKEY

Hockey isn't interesting, and is unfair to black people

SWIMMING

1. That short story by John Cheever, "The Swimmer," I think
2. "Moby Dick"
3. "Go To the Widow-Maker," by James Jones, which has a great underwater masturbation scene

TENNIS

1. John McPhee on Arthur Ashe

ANYTHING BY RED SMITH

Bill Gallo's 12 Greatest Sports Cartoonists

Bill Gallo is the multi-award-winning sports cartoonist of the *New York Daily News* and past president of the Cartoonist Society. Of his selections he says: "The late Willard Mullin (of the *New York World-Telegram & Sun)* is the all-time champ, the greatest sports cartoonist of all time. With modesty, I place myself eighth."

EDITOR'S NOTE: It is modesty, indeed. Most cartoonists, and readers, would place Gallo higher on their lists.

1. Willard Mullin
2. TAD (Thaddeus Aloysius Dorgan)
3. Bob Edgren
4. Leo O'Mealia
5. Burris Jenkins
6. Rube Goldberg
7. Robert Ripley

Willard Mullin executed the greatest sports cartoons.   *Willard Mullin*

A Day at the Races
-by Bill Gallo

Dedicated to all two-dollar bettors.

Bill Gallo's favorite—when the Brinks armored truck was robbed of $1.3 million in Aqueduct Race Track receipts.

Bill Gallo

8. Bill Gallo
9. Ed Hughes
10. Hype Igoe
11. Darvas
12. Pap (Tom Paprocki)

Jim Jacobs' 6 Most Valuable Fight Films

1. Jim Corbett vs. Bob Fitzsimmons, March 17, 1897
2. James Jeffries vs. Tom Sharkey, November 3, 1899
3. Jack Johnson vs. Tommy Burns, December 26, 1908
4. Jack Johnson vs. Jess Willard, April 5, 1915
5. Jack Dempsey vs. Billy Miske, September 6, 1920
6. Gene Tunney vs. Harry Greb, May 23, 1922

SOURCE: Jim Jacobs, vice-president of The Big Fights, Inc., which has a library of more than 17,000 fight films from 1894 to the present and includes 95 percent of all world championship fights on film. Jacobs says, "In my opinion, these six complete, first generation prints are by far the most sought-after in the world."

Ken Regan's 10 Greatest Sports Photographers

Ken Regan, recognized as one of the world's best sports photographers, has photographed virtually every major sporting event, including the Olympic Games, Super Bowl, World Series, Muhammad Ali's fights, and the Stanley Cup. He has been published in *Time, Newsweek, Sports Illustrated,* and *The New York Times,* and has received awards for his photography. He is owner of a photo agency, Camera 5. In making his selections, he overlooked Ken Regan.

1. Neil Leifer
2. Walter Iooss Jr.
3. John Zimmerman

Ken Regan chose this Muhammad Ali-George Foreman shot (in Zaire)
from his collection.

Ken Regan

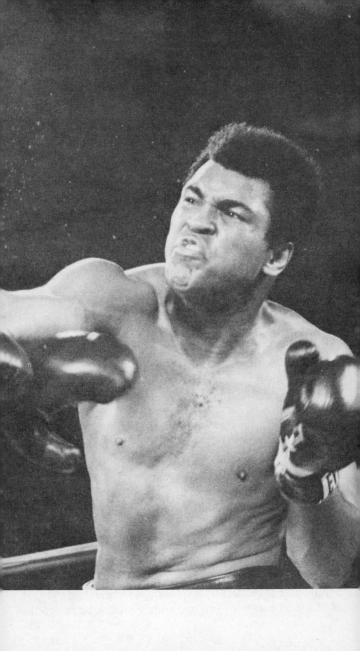

4. Co Rentmeester
5. Rich Clarkson
6. Hy Peskin
7. Art Rickerby
8. George Silk
9. Curt Gunther
10. Richard Meek

James T. Farrell's 10 Favorite Sports Books

Mr. Farrell is the author of the Studs Lonigan Trilogy, a masterpiece and an American classic. He is also a lifetime sports fan. His book on baseball, "My Baseball Diary," belongs on any list of sports books to read. Mr. Farrell notes that his list is not in order of preference.

1. "You Know Me, Al" by Ring Lardner
2. "The Setup," by Joseph Moncure March
3. "Eight Men Out," by Eliot Asinov
4. "The Southpaw," by Mark Harris
5. "The Dodgers," by Tommy Holmes
6. "No Cheering in the Press Box," edited by Jerome Holtzman
7. "My Greatest Day In Baseball," edited by John Carmichael
8. "Babe—A Legend Comes to Life," by Robert W. Creamer
9. "A Man Must Fight," by Gene Tunney
10. "Bang the Drum Slowly," by Mark Harris

Additional comments by Mr. Farrell: "If I had more than ten to list, I should add the book about heavyweight champions written by John Lardner. As you'll see, I have included fiction and Joseph Moncure March's poem, 'The Setup.' But these deal with sports. Incidentally, in the case of March, I mean the original edition. A few years ago, he issued a new edition, in which he watered down the work by changing the dialogue and lines of a Jewish character for fear of being called anti-Semitic. Luigi Pirandello wrote a good novel about a prize fighter, the title of which escapes me. Greatest is a relative word. These books are, at least, all of value, and, I would say, they are worth reading. I have found them so."

Ted Patterson's 10 Sports Firsts in Radio and 10 Sports Firsts in Television

Ted Patterson is an historian of sports broadcasting, having written extensively about radio and TV sports. He is also a collector of sports memorabilia and mementos. As a sportscaster for WBAL in Baltimore, he was three times Maryland sportscaster of the year and is the Voice of Morgan State football.

RADIO

1. First baseball broadcast: August 5, 1921, at Forbes Field, Pittsburgh. KDKA's pioneer announcer, Harold Arlin, described the Pirates' 8-5 victory over the Phillies.
2. First World Series: 1921, three-station hook-up of KDKA in Pittsburgh, WJZ in New York, and WBZ in Boston, from the Polo Grounds. Grantland Rice, famed sports writer, called the action. Graham McNamee began covering the World Series on WEAF in New York in 1923.
3. First prize fight: April 11, 1921, at the Pittsburgh Motor Garden. Florent Gibson, sporting editor of the *Pittsburgh Post,* broadcast the featherweight fight between Johnny Ray and Johnny Dundee, won by Ray in 10 rounds.

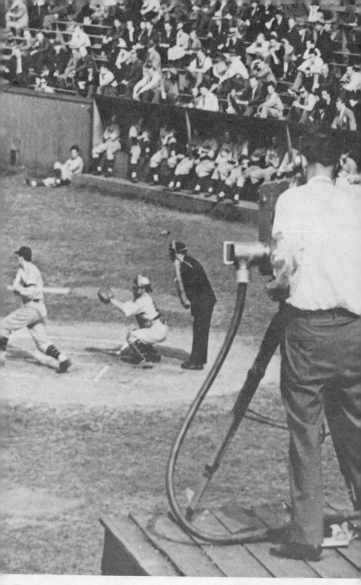

The first televised baseball game—Columbia-Princeton at New York's Baker Field, May 17, 1939.

NBC-TV

4. First heavyweight title fight: July 2, 1921, at Boyle's Thirty Acres in Hoboken, N.J. Champion Jack Dempsey vs. challenger Georges Carpentier. J. Andrew White, with David Sarnoff at his side, described Dempsey's fourth-round knockout. Estimated listening audience: 300,000.

5. First college football broadcast: November 5, 1921, at Forbes Field in Pittsburgh. KDKA's Harold Arlin announced Pitt's 21-13 win over West Virginia. There is also a well-documented tale that on Thanksgiving Day, 1920, the Texas-Texas A&M game was broadcast from College Station by two Aggie cadets, W.A. Tolson and Harry Saunders, over experimental station 5XB.

6. First Rose Bowl broadcast: Alabama-Stanford 7-7 tie in 1927. Graham McNamee on first coast-to-coast hook-up.

7. First Army-Navy broadcast: 1925 at the Polo Grounds, New York. Graham McNamee and Phillips Carlin did the game from Polo Grounds scoreboard while standing on a running board, peering from number opening.

8. First hockey game: March, 1923, in Toronto. Legendary Foster Hewitt broadcast the Toronto Parkdales vs. Kitchener Seniors. U.S. hockey broadcasts began on WEEI in Boston on December 3, 1926.

9. First Indianapolis 500: 1924, WGN in Chicago with Quin Ryan at the microphone. Ryan also broadcast the first Kentucky Derby over WGN in 1925.

10. First athlete-turned-broadcaster: Jack Graney, former Cleveland Indian outfielder from 1908 through 1922, began announcing Indian games in 1932. He stayed on the job through Cleveland's last pennant in 1954. Graney passed away in 1978 at the age of 91.

TELEVISION

1. First televised baseball game: Columbia University hosting Princeton at Baker Field in New York City on May 17, 1939. Bill Stern announced the game, which was the first sporting event ever televised in the United States. There were only 400 sets in the entire country at the time. The station was W2XBS, soon to be WNBC-TV. Princeton won in 10 innings, 2-1.

2. First major league game on TV: August 26, 1939, NBC televised a doubleheader from Ebbets Field between the Dodgers and Cincinnati Reds with Red Barber announcing. The rights fee was a TV set-up in the press room.

3. First college football telecast: September 30, 1939, Fordham vs. Waynesburg in Triboro Stadium on Randalls Island, New York. Bill Stern was the announcer.

4. First televised fight of any kind: Exhibition between Archie Sexton and Laurie Raiteri at the Broadcasting House, London, August 22, 1933.

5. First official TV fight: British light heavyweight title bout between Len Harvey and Jock McAvoy at Harringay Arena in London, August 22, 1933.

6. First televised bout in the United States: Lou Nova–Max Baer from Yankee Stadium over WNBT, June 1, 1939, with Sam Taub the announcer.

7. First coast-to-coast heavyweight title fight: Jersey Joe Walcott vs. Ezzard Charles from Municipal Stadium in Philadelphia, June 5, 1952.

8. First professional football telecast: October 22, 1939, Brooklyn Dodgers over the Philadelphia Eagles, 23-14. Allen "Skip" Walz was the announcer. Ebbets Field was the site.

9. First network World Series telecast: 1947, Brooklyn Dodgers vs. New York Yankees on NBC.

Red Barber with Leo Durocher at Brooklyn's Ebbets Field for the first
major league game on television, August 26, 1939. *NBC-TV*

10. First network college football telecast: Army-Navy in 1945 on four-city hook-up—New York, Philadelphia, Washington, Schenectady—on NBC.

6 Famous Home Run Calls by Announcers

1. "It's going, going, gone."—Mel Allen
2. "Bye-Bye Baby."—Russ Hodges
3. "Goodbye Dolly Grey."—Leo Durocher
4. "Hey, Hey!"—Jack Brickhouse
5. "Open the window, Aunt Minnie."—Rosy Rosewell
6. "Kiss it goodbye."—Bob Prince

Mel Allen calling the shots as New York Yankee announcer. *UPI*

15 Athletes Who Married Actresses or Entertainers

1. Joe DiMaggio   (Marilyn Monroe)
2. Bob Waterfield   (Jane Russell)
3. Leo Durocher   (Laraine Day)
4. Jack Dempsey   (Estelle Taylor)
5. Tom Harmon   (Elyse Knox)
6. Glenn Davis   (Terry Moore)
7. Pancho Gonzalez   (Barbara Darrow)
8. Dan Pastorini   (June Wilkinson)
9. Andy Caray   (Lucy Marlowe)
10. Lance Rentzel   (Joey Heatherton)
11. Rube Marquard   (Blossom Seeley)
12. Terry Bradshaw   (Jo Jo Starbuck)
13. Don Hoak   (Jill Corey)
14. Don Rudolph   (Patti Waggin)
15. Lefty Gomez   (June O'Dea)

28 Athletes Who Became Actors

1. Burt Reynolds   (Florida State football star)
2. Robert Shaw   (English rugby star)
3. Jim Brown   (Hall of Fame pro football star)
4. Dick Gregory   (Track star, Southern Illinois)
5. Johnny Weissmuller   (Olympic swimmer, holder of 10 world records)
6. Johnny Berardino   (11-year major leaguer with St. Louis Browns, Cleveland Indians, Pittsburgh Pirates)
7. Robert Ryan   (Dartmouth heavyweight boxing champion)

Marilyn Monroe and Joe DiMaggio were married on January 14, 1954.

UPI

8. Fred Williamson   (All-pro corner back with Kansas City Chiefs)

9. Bruce Dern   (University of Pennsylvania runner)

10. Mike Connors   (UCLA basketball player)

11. Vince Edwards   (Ohio State swimmer)

12. Johnny Mack Brown   (All-America halfback, U. of Alabama)

13. Woody Strode   (UCLA football star)

14. Kirk Douglas   (St. Lawrence U. wrestling champion)

15. Chuck Connors   (Major leaguer in baseball and basketball)

16. James Garner   (Oklahoma U. football player)

17. John Wayne   (USC lineman)

18. Buster Crabbe   (Olympic swimmer)

19. Jack Palance   (North Carolina U. football player)

20. Canada Lee   (World welterweight contender)

21. Bernie Casey   (NFL defensive halfback)

22. Paul Robeson   (Rutgers U. football star)

23. Ward Bond   (USC football star)

24. Alex Karras   (All-pro NFL tackle)

25. Max Baer   (World's heavyweight boxing champion)

26. Bruce Bennett   (United States discus champ)

27. Maxie Rosenbloom   (World's light heavyweight boxing champion)

28. Alan Ladd   (All-America swimmer and diver)

Burt Reynolds played for Florida State before he played in "The Longest Yard." *Paramount*

Chuck Connors' career took him from baseball (Dodgers, Cubs) and basketball (Rochester Royals, Boston Celtics) to TV stardom as "The Rifleman."

UPI

II

The Good Life

Satchel Paige's 6 Steps
to Eternal Youth

1. Avoid fried meats, which angry up the blood.
2. If your stomach disputes you, lie down and pacify it with cool thoughts.
3. Keep the juices flowing by jangling around gently as you move.
4. Go very light on the vices, such as carrying on in society. The social rumble ain't restful.
5. Avoid running at all times.
6. Don't look back. Something might be gaining on you.

EDITOR'S NOTE: Satchel Paige, called "the greatest pitcher who ever lived" by Dizzy Dean, is the legendary star of baseball's

Satchel Paige warms up as a Kansas City Monarch for game against New York Cubans in Yankee Stadium in 1942. He didn't get a chance to play in the majors until 1948, and he threw in his last big league game for the Kansas City A's in 1965. *UPI*

Negro Leagues. He made the major leagues with the Cleveland Indians in 1949, when he was said to be 42 years old, at least. He pitched three innings for the Kansas City A's in 1965, making him, presumably at age 59, the oldest man to play in the major leagues. Of his six rules, Paige calls No. 6 "My real rule. When you look back, you know how long you've been going and that just might stop you from going any farther. And with me, there was an awful lot to look back on. So I didn't." Paige was elected to the Baseball Hall of Fame in 1971.

Bill Bradley's 6 Favorite Massage Parlors

Bill Bradley, old "Dollar Bill" of the New York Knicks, now sits on Capitol Hill as the junior senator from New Jersey. The senator might have quite a time explaining to his colleagues how, during his playing days, he "had hundreds of massages in health clubs and massage salons in every league city."

EDITOR'S NOTE: It is not uncommon for professional athletes to get massages to rid themselves of the soreness that develops over the course of a rigorous season.

1. Washington Athletic Club, Seattle
2. Phoenix Country Club, Phoenix
3. University Club, Houston
4. Postl's Athletic Club, Chicago
5. International Hotel Health Club, Los Angeles
6. Swedish Massage Institute, New York

SOURCE: *Life On The Run* by Bill Bradley (Quadrangle/The New York Times Book Co.).

10 Quotes on How To Be Ageless in Sports

1. Gordie Howe: "Whatever it is, I don't do it."

Gordie Howe playing at the age of 50 for the New England Whalers.

Steve Babineau

EDITOR'S NOTE: Howe means he doesn't smoke, doesn't drink, doesn't lift anything heavy, and he never—or almost never—does anything extracurricular on the day of a game.

2. Erich Segal: Preparing for a marathon race, "I have my usual pre-race dinner of liver, a bagel, and a hot fudge sundae at Jack and Marian's in Brookline, Mass."

3. Bernard Deacon, holder of 29 world track and field masters records at age 62. "I guess you could say I train on chicken manure. At least everything that grows around here (his organic garden) goes into my diet—mulberries, mangos, papayas, avocados—almost all one's heart desires."

4. Sam Snead: "Golf keeps me going. I play regularly, hardly ever miss a day. I'll do a few little exercises, too, like sit-ups and other stretching drills, but that's just to stay loose."

5. Johnny Green: "Enjoyment. How else could I have played basketball this long? (EDITOR'S NOTE: Green played in the NBA at age 40.) When you feel good, you just want to keep doing it.... You feel like you can keep going forever. It's a certain feeling you get that you really enjoy."

6. Duncan MacLean, 90 years old, former vaudeville performer and record holder in the 100 and 200 meters AAU Masters track and field competition: "I was a dancer by trade. Dancing and running are the same, you know. You have to keep working your muscles."

7. Willie Shoemaker: "A mature person develops a caution that would never have occurred to them years back. Few people with brains will attempt the things they did 20 years ago when they had that grandiose feeling of indestructibility."

8. George Sheehan: "Play is the answer to the puzzle of existence, the stage for our excesses and exuberances."

9. Pancho Gonzalez: "In tennis, it's easier for older guys because there's really no off-season. We don't get way out of condition the way athletes in other sports do."

10. Johnny Weissmuller, former movie Tarzan and Olympic swimming champion, when asked if, at age 72, he was still physically fit: "I still fit into the same size swimming pool I did 40 years ago, don't I?"

George Blanda's 5 Secrets for Longevity

1. Live for today, for tomorrow is not promised to you.

2. No man is ever too old—not if he doesn't want himself to be.

3. Bear Bryant taught me to be tough and to survive. If it hadn't been for him, I probably would have quit when the Chicago Bears tried to retire me in 1959. But I fought back because that's how I was taught.

4. From Betty Blanda: "The secret of his longevity in professional football is handball. He gets on that handball court and plays until a normal human being is ready to drop. If the record for the most hours on the handball court is ever recorded, I know George is going to hold it."

5. Also from Mrs. Blanda: "George watches his diet very carefully. He drinks some, not much. He admits he likes what he calls 'sissy' drinks, grasshoppers and stuff like that. That way you can nurse a drink a long time at a party and nobody pushes booze at you because you have a drink in your hand."

EDITOR'S NOTE: George Blanda played professional football until he was 49 years old and held the all-time NFL record for kicking field goals at the time of his retirement.

Osgood Caruther's 6 Proponents of Anti-Exercise

1. Timothy, New Testament—"For bodily exercise profiteth little; but godliness is profitable unto all things, having promise of life that now is and of that which is to come."

2. Robert Maynard Hutchins—Eminent educator and former president, University of Chicago: "I never run when I can walk. I never sit when I can lie down. Whenever I feel the urge to exercise, I lie down until it goes away."

3. H.L. Mencken—Noted essayist and editor: "I hate all sports as rabidly as a person who likes sports hates common sense."

4. Chauncey Depew—Politician and railroad president: "I get my exercise acting as a pallbearer to my friends who exercise."

5. Dr. Peter J. Steincrohn—Medical doctor, syndicated columnist and author of "How To Be Lazy, Healthy and Physically Fit": "The American obsession with exercise—exercitis—is an iatrogenic disease." (EDITOR'S NOTE: Webster defines this as a disease caused by doctors.)

6. Robert Darling—Noted authority on physical medicine and rehabilitation, when asked how much exercise an office worker needs to keep physically fit: "Fit for what? You're physically fit if your body can get you through your day's work. As for exercise itself, it's been the subject of a lot of nonsense."

SOURCE: The *Los Angeles Times*.

Rusty Staub's 11 Favorite Restaurants in New York City

Rusty Staub specializes in two things—RBIs and good food. He is a noted chef and gourmet and has recently become a restaurateur. His "Rusty's" at 1271 Third Avenue, Manhattan, is fast becoming one of the most popular restaurants in town. In agreeing to pick his favorite New York restaurants, Staub said: "My list is in no order of preference and includes only restaurants I've been to."

1. Ponte's, 39 Desbrosses St.
2. Le Vert-Galant, 109 West 46th St.
3. Il Faro, 325 East 14th St.
4. Sweets, 2 Fulton St.
5. Antolotti's, 337 East 49th St.
6. Cuisine du Coeur, 613 Second Ave.
7. Lutece, 249 East 50th St.
8. Giambelli Fiftieth, 49 East 50th St.
9. Friar's Club, 57 East 55th St.
10. Stage Delicatessen, 834 Seventh Ave.
11. English Pub, 900 Seventh Ave.

15 Well-Known Cigar Smokers in Sports

1. Red Auerbach—He made the cigar a prop, lighting up on the bench when victory was assured for his Boston Celtics. Sometimes he struck his match and began puffing with several minutes left in the game.
2. Jimmy Dykes—Became immortalized as a cigar smoker when, as a player, he failed to slide into third. "I couldn't," he explained. "I carry my cigars in my back pocket and I was afraid I'd break them.".
3. Ralph Houk—Switches from cigars to chewing tobacco once a game starts and back again without hardly missing a beat.
4. Luis Tiant—Cuban cigars, of course.
5. Babe Ruth—Smoked cigars as he did everything else, to excess.
6. Red Holzman—Cigars at breakfast.

Coach Red Auerbach had many a victory cigar with the Boston Celtics.
UPI

Tex Rickard came out of the West with boxing promotions (including a fighter named Jack Dempsey) to rescue the old Madison Square Garden on New York's Madison Avenue. *Joe Val Collection*

 7. Murray Goodman—A nonparticipant in sports, but a
    boxing (and other sports) publicist who is never
    without a stogie.
 8. Tex Rickard—The prototype fast-talking, cigar-
    smoking fight promoter.
 9. Art Rooney—Have you ever seen a picture of the
    owner of the Pittsburgh Steelers in which he did not
    have a cigar in his hand or mouth?
10. Branch Rickey—Churchillian in demeanor, eloquence,
    and always-present cigar, which he used to punctuate
    his oratory.
11. Joe Torre—The humidor on his desk in the Mets'
    clubhouse is always well-stocked.
12. Allie Sherman—Some think he used cigars as an affec-
    tation.
13. Phil King—Former New York Giant running back
    who had an endless source of cigars; he stole them
    from coach Sherman.
14. Sonny Jurgensen—The great quarterback smoked
    them in the clubhouse right up to game time.
15. Johnny Mize—Put his cigar down long enough to hit
    359 career homers, 51 for the New York Giants in
    1947.

4 Distinguished Non-Runners in History

1. Diamond Jim Brady—A top glutton. Never known to
   run a step except towards the men's room.
2. Josef Stalin—Often had runners shot on sight.

3. Socrates—Experimented with running, but found that his toga got in the way, causing frequent spills.
4. Pasquale Nowicki—The city planner who laid out Washington, D.C., in the 18th century.

SOURCE: *The Non-Runners Book*, by Vic Ziegel and Lewis Grossberger (McMillan), dedicated to our 30th President, Calvin Coolidge, who once said, "I choose not to run."

NBA Commissioner Lawrence F. O'Brien's 10 Sports-Minded Presidents

Larry O'Brien, the NBA's third commissioner, served as a key adviser to two presidents (Kennedy and Johnson) and was also a cabinet member in the Johnson administration. As to his own athletic pursuits, O'Brien said in his youth he played a lot of basketball and was nicknamed "Gunner," for what he says were "obvious reasons." He adds that he was an avid watcher during the Kennedys' touch football games.

1. John F. Kennedy—His swimming and sailing prowess were well known through the movie "PT 109," based on his war exploits, and he also enjoyed football, golf, tennis, and his family's touch football matches prior to injuring his back.
2. Jimmy Carter—Plays softball and tennis regularly, fishes, and enjoys watching stock-car racing. Played high school basketball, and ran cross-country.
3. Lyndon B. Johnson—He was a good swimmer, horseman, hunter, and fisherman.

John F. Kennedy as a nine-year-old quarterback for Dexter, the primary grade school he attended in Brookline, Mass. *UPI*

Jimmy Carter takes his turn on the mound in a softball game against the press corps covering his campaign in 1976. *UPI*

4. Harry S. Truman—A tireless walker, he also at times took delight in umpiring ball games.

Harry Truman does calisthenics aboard the USS *Missouri*.

UPI

Teddy Roosevelt *(left)* with brother Elliott in the 1880s.

American Museum of Natural History

5. Franklin D. Roosevelt—Even after becoming an invalid, he kept up with his swimming, horseback riding, and sailing. As a young man, he also skied, tobogganed, and golfed, and stroked an intramural shell in college.

6. Theodore Roosevelt—Perhaps the best amateur athlete to run the country, he enjoyed baseball, lacrosse, polo, fast riding, tennis, and football, although Teddy almost banned the latter because of its roughness at the time. Known for his hunting prowess, he also boxed, swam, rowed, and took long speed walks.

7. Dwight D. Eisenhower—An inveterate golfer during and after his White House days, Ike starred at football and played baseball, up to semi-pro, in his youth. He also liked to fish.

8. Abraham Lincoln—A good horseman, swimmer, crowbar heaver, and master jumper, he also was widely known as being able to outrun, outlift, and outwrestle any man in his home county in Illinois when he was a young man.

9. Gerald R. Ford—A top collegiate football player during his undergraduate days at the University of Michigan, he was his team's captain and later served Yale's varsity as an assistant coach while attending law school. During his Presidency, Ford became known for his golf game, especially among a fast-moving gallery that followed his links' play . . . although not too closely.

10. Woodrow Wilson—He was a devoted, but not very good, golfer who also tried baseball and coached his college football team. Wilson held such a high regard for sports that when his advisers suggested he curtail golf during a critical period, he sneaked off for a game of pool to relieve his pressures.

Until injured, Ike Eisenhower was a promising halfback at West Point.
UPI

NFL Commissioner Pete Rozelle's 10 Greatest Fishing Spots "Where I Have Done Poorly"

1. Kona Coast, Hawaii
2. Spanish Cay, Bahamas
3. Bimini, Bahamas
4. Everglades City, Florida
5. Key West, Florida
6. Marquette, Michigan
7. Boca Grande, Florida
8. Bristol Bay, Alaska
9. Club LaSalle, Canada
10. Montauk, Long Island, New York

EDITOR'S NOTE: Pete Rozelle's favorite recreational sport is tennis.

Ted Williams' 2 Favorite Fishing Holes in the World

"The Splendid Splinter," Ted Williams, the last major league batter to hit .400 (.406 in 1941), is a renowned fisherman who owns more than 5,000 hooks and is on the Sears Roebuck Advisory Board.

1. Miramichi River, Blackville, New Brunswick, Canada (Atlantic salmon)
2. Florida waters off Islamorada in the Florida Keys (bonefish)

EDITOR'S NOTE: The above are listed because his home is Islamorada and he spends winters and most of his springs and falls there, then goes to Blackville in the summer.

The NFL's Pete Rozelle says they all got away.

Pete Rozelle Collection

Says Williams: "During the course of the year, I fish out of a dozen or more of some of the most fabulous fishing spots known to man. It is impossible to list them.

"I can truthfully say that my fishing jaunts have taken me to nearly all parts of the world. I've enjoyed days of fishing in Yucatan, Peru, British Columbia, most of the top places in North and South America. I've thoroughly covered the United States and found some of the best fishing in Wisconsin, and the Florida Keys, as well as Costa Rica, the West Indies, New Zealand, Australia, and others too numerous to mention.

"I enjoy fishing for sailfish, tarpon, trout, bass, and other species, but I have to say that standing in the waters of the Miramichi River, waist-high and in hip boots, waiting for the Atlantic salmon to bite or tug at my line, is my idea of enjoying the leisure life at its very best. The rippling waters, the serenity that surrounds you, offers the greatest relaxation and cleansing of the mind.

"It was in mid-September, 1978, that I caught my 1000th Atlantic salmon out of the Miramichi River. When you consider the fact that the law allows one to catch only two per day, that is rated in fishing circles as an extraordinary feat. I'm mighty proud of it. Also, the fact that I've landed more than 1,000 bonefish is another feat which I look upon with pride. Followers of the legendary Izaak Walton tell me that catching 1,000 or more Atlantic salmon and 1,000 or more bonefish in a life span is comparable to capturing the Triple Crown (batting average, home runs, RBI titles) and the Cy Young Award (the top pitcher in the league) all in one season."

Ted Williams, fishing in Florida in 1947, has no peer as batsman or fisherman.   *UPI*

Malcolm Forbes' 15 Foremost Balloonists

Malcolm Forbes, president and editor-in-chief of *Forbes* magazine, is an internationally known balloonist. He set six world records in hot-air ballooning in 1973 when he became the first person in history to successfully fly coast-to-coast across America in one hot-air balloon. For this achievement, he was awarded the Harmon Trophy as Aeronaut of the Year in 1975. He founded the world's first balloon museum at the Forbes-owned Chateau de Balleroy in Normandy, France. Forbes had originally picked 10 balloonists for his list (treating the Wiederkehr father and two-daughter family as one) but he had to make a new entry on August 17, 1978, when Ben Abruzzo, Maxie Anderson, and Larry Newman, all from Albuquerque, N.M., made the first successful crossing of the Atlantic in a balloon—a 3,200-mile odyssey from Presque Isle, Me., to a French wheat field 50 miles west of Paris. Forbes' selections are in no particular order.

1. Ed Yost—Inventor of many devices that made hot-air ballooning feasible; set the world's distance record in an unsuccessful Atlantic crossing in 1976.
2. Tracy Barns—Established the Balloon Works; is responsible for countless inventions and innovations, and holder of numerous ballooning firsts.
3. Sid Cutter—Organized the first two International Balloon Meets and is responsible for making Albuquerque the ballooning capital of the world.
4. Tom Heinsheimer—World's foremost expert on super-pressure ballooning and scientific use of balloons; built and operates the only Kevlar balloon with its ex-

traordinary potential for use in research and record-setting.

5-7. Wiederkehr Family—Father Matt and daughters Denise and Donna. All are airship pilots. The Wiederkehr women hold many hot-air balloon records.

8. Chauncey Dunn—A Denver sportsman who set an altitude record of 32,949 feet in 1971.

9. Don Cameron—An Englishman who manufactures balloons. Prior to the Americans' successful flight, he was the last to fail in a crossing of the Atlantic, missing by 103 miles. He holds the Montgolfiere Diplome given by the Federation Aeronautique Internationale. Given for best performance and/or contributions to the sport, it's named for the Montgolfiere brothers, who started hot-air ballooning in 1783.

10. Julian Nott—An accomplished English balloonist who organized the 1977 Hot-Air World Championships. He set several altitude and duration records.

11. Fred Dolder—A Swiss who runs over-the-Alps flights each spring and is regarded as the father of Alps ballooning. He has been awarded the Montgolfiere Diplome.

12. Charles Dollfus—A Frenchman considered the "Supreme Balloonist," he has been ballooning for more than 60 years. A recipient of the Montgolfiere Diplome, he has a vast collection of ballooning memorabilia.

13-
15. Ben Abruzzo, Max Anderson, Larry Newman—They were the first to conquer the Atlantic in a balloon. Their six-day flight in Double Eagle II in the summer of 1978 brought them a hero's welcome in France

Ben Abruzzo, Max Anderson, and Larry Newman touch down 50 miles outside Paris in 1978, completing first successful trans-Atlantic balloon crossing.   *UPI*

reminiscent of that given Charles Lindbergh and his Spirit of St. Louis half a century ago.

Jim Jacobs' 6 Greatest Handball Players

The listmaker, Jim Jacobs, has been designated by the *Guinness Book of World Records* as the greatest four-wall player of all time. He won 13 United States Handball Association national titles and, playing with Martin Decatur, was undefeated in doubles competition for 13 years. Jacobs retired from tournament competition at the age of 41 and, quite properly, belongs at the top of the following list.

1. Vic Hershkowitz (Greatest all-around player)
2. Paul Haber (Greatest four-wall player)
3. Steve Sandler (Greatest one-wall player)
4. Martin Decatur (Greatest all-around doubles player, one-wall, three-wall, four-wall)
5. Oscar Obert (Greatest all-around shotmaker, one-wall, three-wall, four-wall)
6. Freddie Lewis (Five-time national four-wall singles champion and heir apparent to many of the "greatest" titles listed above)

Jacobs notes: "I have played against or watched all of these men. I have not played against Joe Platak, who was a great player long before my time, in 1935. Thus, I did not rank Joe because I don't want to use hearsay."

Wilt Chamberlain's All-Time Men's and Women's Volleyball Teams

Wilt "The Stilt" Chamberlain, the greatest scorer in NBA history, holds the title of President, International

Wilt Chamberlain is a volleyball star, too.   *Doug Badt Collection*

Volleyball Association. He is an avid volleyball player and, at 7-1, an obviously good one. He played for the Orange County Stars in 1977 and in 1978 was named co-MVP in the all-star match at El Paso. He frequently plays two-man volleyball in Southern California and in Hawaii.

MEN'S TEAM (all indoors)

1. Garth Pischke
2. Ed Skorek
3. Jon Roberts
4. Stan Gosciniak
5. Bebeto DeFreitas
6. Dodge Parker

WOMEN'S TEAM (some indoors, some beach)

1. Kathy Gregory
2. Gerrie McGahan
3. Rosie Wegrich
4. Mary Jo Peppler
5. Flo Hyman
6. Mikki McFadden

EDITOR'S NOTE: Wilt Chamberlain places himself as an alternate on either the men's or women's team.

Mort Leve's Top 10 Handball Players

1. Joe Platak
2. Jim Jacobs
3. Al Banuet
4. Vic Hershkowitz
5. Paul Haber
6. Fred Lewis
7. Sam Atcheson
8. Maynard Laswell

9. John Sloan
10. Steve Sandler

EDITOR'S NOTE: Mort Leve is executive secretary of the United States Handball Association.

Bonnie J. Cardone's 10 Best Skin-Diving Sites in the World

1. Red Sea
2. Truk Lagoon
3. Palancar Reef
4. Cayman Islands
5. San Salvador Island
6. Bonaire
7. Belize
8. Lanaii, Hawaii
9. British Virgin Islands
10. Roatan

EDITOR'S NOTE: Bonnie J. Cardone is senior editor of *Skin Diver* magazine.

Jack Lewis' 10 Most Influential People in Archery History, Fact or Fiction

1. Robin Hood—Best-known hood in history.
2. William Tell—Noted for apples and overtures.
3. Howard Hill—Famous bowhunter and trick shooter. Brought archery to Hollywood.
4. Fred Bear—Famous bowhunter; started the first (and still largest) major archery manufacturing company.
5. James D. Easton—Developer of the aluminum arrow shaft.
6. Saxton Pope—Forefather of modern bowhunting (Pope and Young Club).

7. Art Young—Forefather of modern bowhunting (Pope and Young Club).
8. H.W. Allen—Inventor of the compound bow.
9. Cupid.
10. One Way—The road sign that did little for the bow, but immortalized the arrow.

EDITOR'S NOTE: Jack Lewis is editor of *Bow & Arrow* magazine.

Willis Reed's 8 Favorite Hunting Places

Willis Reed, former great center for the New York Knicks and later coach of the NBA team, is a renowned hunter. He spends much of his leisure time at his favorite pasttime. The following list is in no order of preference.

1. Sullivan County, N.Y. (Deer with bow, and turkey, in the spring)
2. Delaware County, N.Y. (Deer with bow, and turkey, in the spring)
3. Bradford, Pa. (Deer with bow, and turkey, in the spring.)
4. Tioga, Pa. (Deer with bow, and turkey, in the spring)
5. Jackson Hole, Wyo. (Elk and black bear)
6. Kodiak Island, Alaska (Kodiak bear)
7. Wheelock, Vt. (Black bear with bow)
8. Northern La. (Rabbit, with beagles, and deer)

20 Athletes Who Were 'Rhodes Scholars

Named for Cecil Rhodes, a British colonial pioneer and statesman, Rhodes scholarships have been awarded since

(Above) Byron "Whizzer" White as a Colorado University halfback in 1937; *(below)* as an Associate Justice of the Supreme Court *(seated, far right)* in 1972. *University of Colorado, UPI*

1904. They provide for two years of study at the University of Oxford in England and are given on the basis of these criteria: literary and scholastic achievement; fondness for and success in sports; character; and leadership.

1. J. W. Fulbright, football, Arkansas, 1925
2. F. Tremaine Billings, football, Princeton, 1933
3. Howard K. Smith, track, Tulane, 1937
4. Byron "Whizzer" White, football and basketball, Colorado, 1938
5. Frank Tatum, golf, Stanford, 1947
6. Malcolm McLane, skiing, Dartmouth, 1948
7. Ham Richardson, tennis, Tulane, 1955
8. George Munroe, basketball, Dartmouth, 1949
9. Pete Dawkins, football, West Point, 1949
10. John Wideman, basketball, Penn, 1963
11. Bill Bradley, basketball, Princeton, 1965
12. Heyward Dotson, basketball, Columbia, 1970
13. Willie Bogan, football, Dartmouth, 1971
14. Tom Neville, football, Yale, 1971
15. Terence Valenzuela, fencing, Harvard, 1973
16. Misha Petkevich, figure skating, Harvard, 1973
17. Tom McMillen, basketball, Maryland, 1974
18. Kenneth Brown, rowing, Cornell, 1974
19. Pat Haden, football, USC, 1975
20. Caroline Alexander,* pentathlon, Florida State, 1978

*It was not until 1977 that Rhodes scholarships were awarded to women.

(Opposite, above) Bill Bradley strikes uncharacteristic stance as a New York Knick against Golden State's Rick Barry in 1975. *(Below)* In 1978 the Rhodes Scholar was elected to the U.S. Senate from New Jersey.   *UPI*

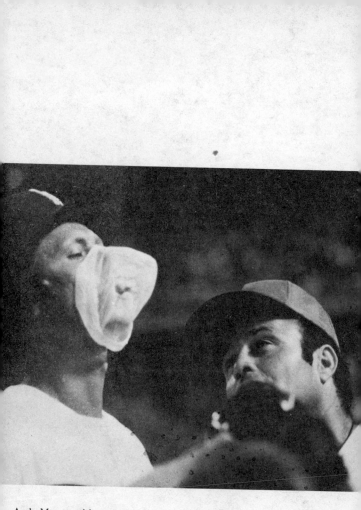

Andy Messersmith once won a bubble gum title, but he didn't make Joe Garagiola's *(right)* all-star team.

III

Balls and Strikes

Joe Garagiola's All-Star Bubble-Gum-Blowing Baseball Team

First base—Ed Goodson, San Francisco Giants, 10½"
Second base—Bill Madlock, Chicago Cubs, 8½"
Shortstop—Lee Richard, Chicago White Sox, 8½"
Third base—George Brett, Kansas City Royals, 14½"
Outfield—Walt Williams, New York Yankees, 16"
Outfield—Joe Lovitto, Texas Rangers, 16"
Outfield—Rick Miller, Boston Red Sox, 13"
Catcher—Johnny Oates, Philadelphia Phillies, 21"
Left-handed pitcher—Mike Cosgrove, Houston Astros, 14"
Right-handed pitcher—Eric Raich, Cleveland Indians, 21"
Designated hitter—Kurt Bevacqua, Milwaukee Brewers, 17½"

Pitchers and catchers blow bigger bubbles than any other position.

Raich, after qualifying for team championship, was sent to the minor leagues.

Raich, asked if he ever had any problems blowing bubbles, said: "Once a bubble busted and pulled out a contact lens."

Bevacqua used candle wax so gum would not stick to his mustache.

Catfish Hunter lost the team title to Walt Williams and complained, "I would have won the damn thing except they busted my bubble trying to measure it."

SOURCE: Sy Berger, VP, Topps Bubble Gum Co., Inc., which sponsored the Bazooka/Joe Garagiola Big League Bubble Gum Blowing Championship, 1976.

Commissioner Bowie Kuhn's 10 Greatest Baseball Thrills

1. The Miracle Mets of 1969.
2. Brooks Robinson's play in the 1970 World Series.
3. Roberto Clemente's performance in the 1971 World Series.
4. Henry Aaron's 714th and 715th home runs.
5. Lou Brock's stolen base feats—118 in a single season (and in 1977, 893 for a career, surpassing Ty Cobb's modern record).
6. The 1975 World Series, particularly the sixth game.
7. The "Fidrych Syndrome"—the remarkable interaction between fans and players, which started to happen frequently in 1976 and has provided a happy scene ever since.
8. Reggie Jackson's four consecutive home runs in the 1977 World Series.
9. Pete Rose's 44-game consecutive hitting streak in 1978.

Henry Aaron has the ball he hit for No. 715 to break Babe Ruth's home run record.

UPI

10. The Yankees' comeback in 1978.

EDITOR'S NOTE: Commissioner Kuhn limited his "thrills" to events that took place on the playing field during his time as commissioner. His choices are listed chronologically and not in order of preference, because "it would be extremely difficult to say which event has been the most pleasing."

Ron LeFlore's 10 Greatest Stealers

The speedy centerfielder of the Detroit Tigers led the American League in stolen bases in 1978 and set a league record the same year when he swiped 27 consecutive bases without being thrown out. He is the subject of a CBS television movie, "One in a Million," based on his book, "Breakout," that details his life, from prison (for stealing, of course) to the major leagues.

1. Lou Brock
2. Maury Wills
3. Joe Morgan
4. Ron LeFlore
5. Luis Aparicio
6. Ty Cobb
7. Freddie Fruit—"That's just his nickname. I don't know his real name. I never had the nerve to ask him. But he was a great stealer. He never got caught."
8. Willie Mays
9. Butch Berry—"He was a born thief. He was my boyhood idol. He could steal anything—and he did."
10. Rusty Staub—"If he could run, he would have been great because he really knows how to steal bases."

When Ron LeFlore talks about thievery, he rates Lou Brock at the head of the list.
           UPI

Jack Lang's 12 Worst Deals
in Baseball History

Jack Lang, secretary-treasurer of the Baseball Writers Association of America, has been watching baseball trades, the good and the bad, for three decades as a baseball writer for the *Long Island Press* and *New York News*.

1. Christy Mathewson for Amos Rusie
2. Sparky Lyle for Danny Cater
3. Nolan Ryan for Jim Fregosi
4. Rogers Hornsby for Shanty Hogan
5. Gaylord Perry and Frank Duffy for Sam McDowell
6. George Foster for Frank Duffy
7. Red Ruffing for Cedric Durst
8. Rusty Staub for Donn Clendenon and Jesus Alou (When Clendenon failed to report, he was replaced in the trade by Jack Billingham and Skip Guinn.)
9. Rusty Staub for Mickey Lolich
10. Ken Singleton and Mike Torrez for Dave McNally, Bill Kirkpatrick, and Rich Coggins
11. Joe Morgan, Jack Billingham, Cesar Geronimo, Ed Armbrister, and Denis Menke for Lee May, Tommy Helms, and Jimmy Stewart.
12. Amos Otis for Joe Foy

Jack Lang says: "It is difficult to single out any one deal as the worst ever made. But the one the Reds consummated with the Giants in 1900 will do until something worse comes along. The Reds swapped Christy Mathewson for Amos Rusie, who had won 241 games for New York before the turn of the century. Mathewson went on to win 367 games, all but one for the Giants. Rusie never won a game for the Reds.

"Dick O'Connell, former Boston general manager, openly admitted 'The worst deal I ever made was Lyle for Cater.' Cater did little for the Red Sox, while Lyle became a premier relief pitcher and Cy Young Award winner for the Yankees.

"Two men twice figured in 'worst deals.' Rusty Staub went from Houston to Montreal for Donn Clendenon, who never reported to Houston while Staub became a star with the Expos and later with the Mets. Staub was later dealt by the Mets to Detroit for Mickey Lolich, who quit after one season while Staub continued to hammer in runs for the Tigers.

"Frank Duffy was also included in a pair of lulus. He went from the Reds with minor league pitcher Vern Geishert to the Giants for Foster, who became the National League home run king. Duffy later went with Gaylord Perry to the Indians for Sam McDowell. Perry became one of the winningest pitchers in baseball history, pitching past his 40th birthday, while McDowell faded into oblivion.

"In their short history, the Mets have made more than their share of bum deals. Besides the Staub-for-Lolich stinker, they also gave up strikeout king Nolan Ryan for fat and aging Jim Fregosi. It was also the Mets who sent Amos Otis to the Royals for Joe Foy. Otis became the great Kansas City centerfielder, while Foy, who had personal problems, left the Mets after one dismal season."

Monte Irvin's All-Time Negro*
All-Star Team

First base—Buck Leonard, Homestead Grays
Second base—Sammy T. Hughes, Baltimore Elite Giants

*"We were Negroes then," says Hall of Famer Monte Irvin, who, long before he became a hero of the New York Giants, was a star of the Newark Eagles. They played in the Negro National and Negro American leagues, and Monte, mostly an infielder then, played in the legaue from 1937 through 1948 (with time out for Army duty in Europe during World War II). Monte signed with the Giants for $5,000 in 1949. "I took a cut from what I was making at Newark," Monte says. "But it was time." The rest is history.

Third base—Ray Dandridge, Newark Eagles
Shortstop—Willie Wells, Newark Eagles
Left field—Martin Dihigo, New York Cubans
Center field—Cool Papa Bell, St. Louis Stars
Right field—Bill Wright, Baltimore Elite Giants
Catcher—Josh Gibson, Homestead Grays
Right-handed pitcher—Satchel Paige, Kansas City Monarchs
Left-handed pitcher—Slim Jones, Philadelphia Stars
Manager—Rube Foster, Chicago American Giants

The 10 Greatest Firemen

Firemen wear red suspenders and they also come into a baseball game when the situation is desperate. Relief pitchers have sprung into prominence only within the last 20 years. Pat McDonough, a sportswriter for the old *New York World-Telegram & Sun* whose hobby is baseball statistics, provided the statistics for this list. He notes that Firpo Marberry was a relief specialist for the Washington Senators in the 1920s, and his teammate was Walter Johnson, considered the greatest pitcher of all time. McDonough also notes that Johnny Murphy, a relief pitcher not on the list, finished so many games for Lefty Gomez with the Yankees in the 30s and 40s, "people thought his name was Gomez-Murphy."

1. Fred "Firpo" Marberry—First relief specialist with Washington in 1920s.
2. Hoyt Wilhelm—Relieved in 1,002 games with nine teams in two leagues and has the most relief wins in history, 123.
3. Elroy Face—Had 657 consecutive relief appearances

Hall of Famer Josh Gibson of the Homestead Grays was known as the black Babe Ruth. *UPI*

without a start, a record; had the most relief victories in the National League, 96; and the most relief victories in a single season, 18.

4. Hugh Casey—Best career winning percentage for a fireman, .718; relieved in six games in the 1947 World Series.

5. Rollie Fingers—Seven consecutive seasons of 60 or more games and 20 or more saves; holds the record for most World Series saves, 6.

6. Jim Konstanty—The first relief pitcher to win Most Valuable Player award, with Philadelphia Phillies in 1950.

7. Mike Marshall—Relieved in 106 games with Los Angeles Dodgers in 1974 and in 198 games over two seasons, 1973 and 1974; first relief pitcher to win Cy Young Award, 1974.

8. Sparky Lyle—More than 1,000 innings in relief for the Boston Red Sox and New York Yankees; second relief pitcher, and first in the American League, to win Cy Young Award, 1977.

9. John Hiller—Most saves in a season, 38 for the Detroit Tigers in 1973.

10. Luis Arroyo—Finished 44 winning games for the New York Yankees in 1961.

Hoyt Wilhelm's 5 Tips for Knuckleballers

1. Don't try to throw the knuckleball as an adult, unless you threw it as a kid.

2. Don't try to be a part-time knuckleball pitcher; there ain't no such animal.

The Brooklyn Dodgers' Hugh Casey won two games as a fireman in the 1947 World Series against the Yankees, who took it in seven.   *UPI*

3. Never let the ball spin. It won't if you throw it overhand and straight without breaking the wrist.
4. Throw every day.
5. Don't panic if your knuckler isn't working today; it will come back tomorrow.

Henry Aaron's 5 Ways To Beat Babe Ruth's Record

1. Eat one large meal a day.
2. Smoke only six cigarettes daily.
3. Cultivate the ability to take catnaps—on planes, buses, etc.
4. Waste no energy.
5. Compensate for age when playing. (Was right fielder, moved to left field to prevent undue strain on weakened throwing arm; dropped bat lower and moved it closer to his chest in an effort to cut down on big swing, which left him with a nagging backache.)

The 7 Commandments of George Steinbrenner

"Actually," argues the principal owner of the New York Yankees, "they are not commandments at all, and they aren't even mine."

Steinbrenner said the commandments are Gabe Paul's, and they came about when Paul was president of the Yankees and Steinbrenner was about to fire Billy Martin for the umptyumpth time. Billy was to be fired (resigned, the Yankees said) a year later; then he was unresigned five days after that for delivery two years later.

"Gabe," asked Steinbrenner, bowing to Paul's 50 years in the game, "what makes a good manager?"

Paul took a piece of paper and wrote down his answer.

"That's good," said Steinbrenner. "May I have that?"

Paul said he could and Steinbrenner folded it and placed it in his pocket, where it remained until later that afternoon when he was talking with some newsmen.

"What do you look for in a manager?" asked one of the newsmen.

Funny he should ask, said Steinbrenner, as he pulled the paper out of his pocket and asked Gabe Paul for permission to impart his wisdom to the newsmen.

"And that," said Steinbrenner, "is how the Seven Commandments came about."

Nevertheless, they will go down as Steinbrenner's Seven Commandments, and he's stuck with them.

1. Does he win?
2. Does he work hard enough?
3. Is he emotionally equipped to lead men?
4. Is he organized?
5. Does he understand human nature?
6. Is he prepared for each game?
7. Is he honorable?

Dan Daniel's 10 Most Frequently Asked Baseball Questions

Dan Daniel was the dean of American baseball writers until his retirement in the late 1960s, following the demise of his newspaper, the *New York World-Telegram & Sun*.

His "Ask Dan" column was one of the most popular features in the newspaper, and he agreed to prepare this list of 10 most frequently asked questions, with answers in parentheses.

1. Has anybody hit a fair ball out of Yankee Stadium? (No.)
2. Who holds the record for hitting safely in consecutive

games? (Joe DiMaggio, who hit in 56 consecutive games in 1941.)

3. What is the record for playing in the most consecutive games? (Lou Gehrig's 2,130 consecutive games from 1923 to 1939.)

4. Did any pitcher ever pitch no-hitters in consecutive appearances? (Just one, Johnny VanderMeer, who pitched no-hitters in consecutive appearances for Cincinnati against Boston on June 11, 1938, and against Brooklyn on June 15, 1938.)

5. Who pitched the greatest number of no-hitters? (Sandy Koufax, Los Angeles Dodgers, and Nolan Ryan, California Angels, each have pitched four no-hit games.)

6. Who hit the greatest number of home runs in his career? (Henry Aaron, who hit 755 home runs for Milwaukee and Atlanta [NL] and Milwaukee [AL].)

7. Who hit the greatest number of home runs for times at bat in his career? (Babe Ruth, who hit 714 career home runs, or one every 11.75 times at bat.)

8. Who hit the greatest number of home runs in a single season? (Roger Maris, who hit 61 home runs in 1961, during a 162-game season. For a 154-game season, the record belongs to Babe Ruth, who hit 60 home runs in 1927.)

9. Which infielder had the greatest number of consecutive errorless games? (Including first basemen, the record is 178 consecutive errorless games by Mike Hegan of Milwaukee and Oakland [AL] from Sept. 24, 1970, through May 20, 1973. Excluding first basemen, it's Jim Davenport, San Francisco third baseman, who played in 97 consecutive errorless games from July 29, 1966, through April 28, 1968.)

10. Who was the Most Valuable Player of a major league most often? (Six players have won three Most Valuable

Player awards—Jimmy Foxx, Joe DiMaggio, Yogi Berra and Mickey Mantle in the American League; Roy Campanella and Stan Musial in the National League. (EDITOR'S NOTE: The Baseball Writers Association of America did not begin naming a Most Valuable Player until 1931.)

Pete Rose's 6 Toughest Pitchers

1. Jim Brewer
2. Tommy John
3. Randy Jones
4. Sandy Koufax
5. Juan Marichal
6. Bob Gibson

When you have collected over 3,000 hits and have the modern National League record for hitting in 44 consecutive games, the list can't be too long.

Says Rose: "Brewer was the toughest. He frustrated me. Brewer and Jones were the only two pitchers I didn't switch hit against. I batted lefty against them because I couldn't hit them right-handed. Brewer still got me out with screwballs.

"Koufax was the hardest thrower, Marichal the best pitcher—he could throw six pitches—and Gibson was the best competitor I ever faced."

Walter Alston's All-Time Dodger Team

Walter Alston was an unknown with only one major league at-bat when he was named to succeed Charlie Dressen as manager of the Brooklyn Dodgers in 1954. He stayed for 23 one-year contracts, winning over 2,000 major league games, more than any manager in history except Connie

Mack, John McGraw, Joe McCarthy, and Bucky Harris. He retired after the 1976 season and agreed to select his all-time Dodger team for *The Complete Handbook of Baseball.* It follows:

First base—Gil Hodges
Second base—Jim Gilliam
Third base—Jackie Robinson
Shortstop—PeeWee Reese
Left field—Sweet Lou Johnson
Center field—Duke Snider
Right field—Carl Furillo
Catcher—Roy Campanella
Pitchers—Sandy Koufax
          Don Drysdale
          Don Sutton
          Don Newcombe
          Carl Erskine
          Clem Labine
          Ron Perranoski
          Jim Brewer

25 Major League Baseball Players Who Were Born in Europe

1. Honest John Anderson—Sasbourg, Norway
2. Jimmy Archer—Dublin, Ireland
3. Rugger Ardizoia—Oleggio, Italy
4. Jimmy Austin—Swansea, Wales
5. Heinz Becker—Berlin, Germany
6. Bob Belloir—Heidelberg, Germany
7. Reno Bertoia—St. Vito Uldine, Italy
8. Hank Biasetti—Beano, Italy
9. Bert Blyleven—Zeist, Holland
10. Dave Brain—Hereford, England
11. Al Campanis—Kos, Greece

12. Moe Drabowsky—Ozanna, Poland
13. Olaf Hendriksen—Kirkerup, Denmark
14. Otto Hess—Berne, Switzerland
15. Kurt Krieger—Traisen, Austria
16. Axel Lindstrom—Gustafsburg, Sweden
17. John Michaelson—Tivalkoski, Finland
18. Fritz Mollwitz—Kolberg, Germany
19. Marino Pieretti—Lucca, Italy
20. Rube Schauer—Odessa, Russia
21. Harry Smith—Yorkshire, England
22. Bobby Thomson—Glasgow, Scotland
23. Elmer Valo—Ribnik, Czechoslovakia
24. Jimmy Walsh—Killila, Ireland
25. Jimmy Wiggs—Trondhjeim, Norway

Leo Durocher's 11 Greatest Umpires

In his half-century in baseball, as a player, coach, and manager, colorful, controversial, fiery Leo Durocher had his share of arguments with umpires. Still, he respects and recognizes the job umpires do and agreed to submit his list of the greatest umpires of all time.

1. Bill Klem
2. Al Barlick
3. Dolly Stark
4. Tom Gorman
5. Shag Crawford
6. Doug Harvey
7. Bruce Froemming
8. Chris Pelakoudas
9. Ed Vargo
10. Ed Sudol
11. Billy Williams

Leo Durocher adds: "In my opinion, these are the best ones, but it's only my personal opinion. I don't like to rate them, but these were the best while I was around. I chose all National Leaguers because I don't know the American League that well."

Bob Feller's 10 Most Beautiful Minor League Ballparks

The great Hall of Fame fireballer of the Cleveland Indians spends a good deal of time touring minor league cities, where he is in great demand for personal appearances.

1. Bluefield, West Virginia
2. Little Falls, New York
3. Helena, Montana
4. Midland, Texas
5. Salinas, California
6. Rochester, New York
7. Columbus, Ohio
8. Albuquerque, New Mexico
9. Denver, Colorado
10. Honolulu, Hawaii

Bob Feller notes: "Denver and Honolulu are also used for football. No minor league park was considered that is spring training headquarters for a major league club. If I were allowed to list more than 10, I would add Gastonia, N.C.; Nashville, Tenn.; Jackson, Miss.; and Vancouver, B.C., Canada."

New York Giants manager Leo Durocher has just been tossed out of a 1949 game against the Cardinals. The umpire, Larry Goetz, did not make Leo's list of greatest umpires.   *UPI*

The 13 Easiest Home Run Areas
in Major League History

1. Polo Grounds, right field
2. Baker Bowl, right field
3. Fenway Park, left field
4. Polo Grounds, left field
5. Ebbets Field, left field
6. League Park, right field
7. Los Angeles Coliseum, left field
8. Old Yankee Stadium, right field
9. Forbes Field, left field ("Kiner's Corner")
10. Shibe Park, left field
11. Sportsman's Park, right field (with the screen down)
12. Atlanta, any field
13. Wrigley Field, any field (with the wind blowing out)

EDITOR'S NOTE: Interestingly, Polo Grounds, New York; Ebbets Field, Brooklyn; League Park, Cleveland; L.A. Coliseum; Forbes Field, Pittsburgh; Shibe Park, Philadelphia; and Sportsman's Park, St. Louis, are no longer in existence. And Yankee Stadium has been remodeled.

SOURCE: Red Foley.

The 10 Toughest Home Run Areas
in Major League History

1. Polo Grounds, center field
2. Old Yankee Stadium, center field
3. Forbes Field, center field
4. Los Angeles Coliseum, center field
5. Forbes Field, left field
6. Yankee Stadium, left field
7. Busch Stadium, any field
8. Oakland Coliseum, any field

9. Griffith Stadium, left field
10. Texas Stadium, right field

SOURCE: Red Foley.

Baseball's 9 Toughest Strikeouts of All Time

	At-Bats Per Strikeout
1. Joe Sewell	62.56
2. Lloyd Waner	44.92
3. Nellie Fox	42.74
4. Tommy Holmes	40.92
5. Andy High	33.85
6. Sam Rice	33.71
7. Frankie Frisch	33.50
8. Frank McCormick	30.28
9. Don Mueller	29.89

EDITOR'S NOTE: Ratings are based on a minimum of 4,000 at-bats. Strikeout records were not kept prior to 1913, therefore records of Wee Willie Keeler, Lave Cross, Tris Speaker and Stuffy McInnis—who would make the Top 9—are incomplete and not listed.

SOURCE: The Elias Baseball Bureau.

Baseball's 15 Easiest Strikeouts of All Time

	At-Bats Per Strikeout
1. Reggie Jackson	3.93
2. Bobby Bonds	4.01
3. Dick Allen	4.07
4. Donn Clendenon	4.08
5. Willie Stargell	4.10

6.	Rick Monday	4.14
7.	Woodie Held	4.26
8.	Frank Howard	4.44
9.	Deron Johnson	4.51
10.	Jimmy Wynn	4.64
11.	Mickey Mantle	4.74
12.	Harmon Killebrew	4.80
13.	Lee May	4.89
14.	Doug Rader	4.91
15.	Bob Allison	4.92

EDITOR'S NOTE: Ratings are based on 4,000 at-bats and are complete through the 1977 season.

SOURCE: The Elias Sports Bureau.

Tito Fuentes' 4 Biggest Hot Dogs

1. Willie Montanez
2. Tito Fuentes
3. Jose Cardenal
4. Reggie Jackson

Tito Fuentes, who played with the San Francisco Giants, San Diego Padres, and Detroit Tigers, proudly states that when Montanez and Cardenal were asked for their list, they both placed Tito first.

"I'm kind of a clown," says Fuentes, who bounces his bat off home plate, twirls it behind his back like a majorette, and keeps up a steady stream of chatter with the catcher and plate umpire. "I'm proud of myself. Some people say, 'How can you play and at the same time be talking with umpires and every player and concentrate on the sign the catcher is giving?' But I can do it. I have to have talk and fun in my job; otherwise it's just a job."

Reggie Jackson, fanning here for the Oakland A's, has a strikeout record that he'd be happy to relinquish.   *UPI*

Montanez, who plays first base with a flair, is known for pointing at the ball after he has smashed it for a base hit. Cardenal also plays with a flourish. Jackson's place on the list was secured by former Oakland teammate Darold Knowles, who once said of Reggie: "There isn't enough mustard in the world to cover that hot dog."

All-Time Listing of the Top Home Run Hitters Whose Names Begin With Each Letter of the Alphabet, 1900–1978

A—Henry Aaron, 755
B—Ernie Banks, 512
C—Orlando Cepeda, 379
D—Joe DiMaggio, 361
E—Del Ennis, 288
F—Jimmy Foxx, 534
G—Lou Gehrig, 493
H—Frank Howard, 382
I—Monte Irvin, 99
J—Reggie Jackson, 340
K—Harmon Killebrew, 573
L—Ernie Lombardi, 190
M—Willie Mays, 660
N—Graig Nettles, 244
O—Mel Ott, 511
P—Boog Powell, 339
Q—Jamie Quirk and Frank Quilici, 5
R—Babe Ruth, 714
S—Willie Stargell, 429
T—Frank Thomas, 286
U—Del Unser, 81
V—Mickey Vernon, 172
W—Ted Williams, 521
X—

Y—Carl Yastrzemski, 383
Z—Gus Zernial, 237

EDITOR'S NOTE: There has never been a major league player whose last name began with the letter "X"; closest race was among the Cs, Cepeda (379) beating out Norm Cash (377) and Rocky Colavito (374).

All-Time Listing of the Winningest Pitchers Whose Names Begin With Each Letter of the Alphabet, 1900–1978

A—Grover Cleveland Alexander, 373
B—Mordecai "Three Finger" Brown, 239
C—Stan Coveleski, 216
D—Paul Derringer, 223
E—Howard Ehmke, 167
F—Bob Feller, 266
G—Lefty Grove, 300
H—Carl Hubbell, 253
I—Ham Iburg, 11
J—Walter Johnson, 416
K—Jim Kaat, 261
L—Ted Lyons, 260
M—Christy Mathewson, 373
N—Bobo Newsom, 211
O—Claude Osteen, 196
P—Ed Plank, 325
Q—Jack Quinn, 241
R—Robin Roberts, 286
S—Warren Spahn, 363
T—Luis Tiant, 204
U—George Uhle, 200
V—Dazzy Vance, 197
W—Early Wynn, 300
X—

Y—Cy Young, 511
Z—Tom Zachary, 185

Marty Appel's 10 Members of the Baseball Hall of Fame Who Don't Belong

1. Rabbit Maranville—His statistics (a lifetime batting average of .258) do not measure up to others of his era and position.
2. Tommy McCarthy—He got in through linkage, riding the coattails of Hugh Duffy, with whom he made up "The Heavenly Twins" of the Boston National League Club in the 1890s.
3. Harry Hooper—Another beneficiary of linkage—with Tris Speaker.
4. Roger Bresnahan—Christy Mathewson's catcher: big deal. He also was credited with inventing shin guards and chest protector. Another big deal. If you get hit with enough foul balls, eventually you'll invent some protection. Does that mean Steve Yeager belongs in the Hall of Fame for inventing the flap that protects his neck?
5. Martin Dihigo—No doubt a good pitcher, but he barely scratched out 10 years in the Negro Leagues.
6. Bucky Harris—Just an average major league manager who happened to hang around a long time and got fame by winning the 1924 American League pennant with Washington at the age of 24.
7. Morgan G. Bulkeley—The first National League president, but a joke. He served only one year, largely as a figurehead. But when they inducted Ban Johnson, the first American League president, who belongs, they figured they might as well put in the first National League president as well.

8-10. Tinker-Evers-Chance—The famed double play combination of Joe Tinker, Johnny Evers, and Frank Chance, who made it only because they were immortalized in a poem by Franklin P. Adams, who deserves to be in the Hall of Fame more than they do.

Marty Appel's 10 Who Belong in Baseball's Hall of Fame But Aren't

1. Ernie Lombardi—A lifetime .306 hitter and a catcher who batted over .300 10 times and won two batting titles.

2. Johnny Mize—A lifetime .312 hitter with 359 career home runs and 1,337 career RBI.

3. Ned Hanlon—Managed 15 Hall of Famers, and was winner of five pennants in seven seasons from 1894 through 1900.

4. Rube Foster—Many consider him the best pitcher of the Negro Leagues, as good as, if not better than, Satchel Paige.

5-6. Phil Rizzuto and PeeWee Reese—Linked because were the dominant shortstops on the dominant teams in the 1940s and '50s.

7. Chuck Klein—A lifetime batting average of .320, 300 home runs, four league home run titles.

8. Arky Vaughan—A lifetime .318 hitter as a shortstop and the NL batting champion in 1935 with a .385 average.

9. Bowie Kuhn—Brought new powers to the office of the commissioner in attempts to preserve the balance of power.

10. Marvin Miller—Director of the Players Association. He has made a significant contribution to the game,

which, after all, is what the Hall of Fame should recognize; it should not be merely the establishment's domain.

Marty Appel is the author of *Baseball's Best: The Hall of Fame Gallery* (McGraw-Hill).

IV

The Name Game

All-Time Baseball Teams That Politicians, Statespeople, and Other Celebrities Might Have Chosen

"Mr. President, as the nation's No. 1 baseball fan, would you be willing to name your all-time baseball team?"

When President Nixon not only said he would, but did, and made the sports pages of just about every newspaper in the country with his selection, that was an open invitation for everybody to get into the act.

In the interest of fair play, it seems only right that others be given equal time.

What follows are the teams politicians, statespeople, and other celebrities might have chosen if they had the time, the inclination, and opportunity. The selections are hypothetical, but the players chosen are real people who actually played in the major leagues.

LEONID BREZHNEV

First base—Lefty O'Doul
Second base—Red Schoendienst

Third base—Red Rolfe
Shortstop—Pinky May
Outfield—Eric "The Red" Tipton
Outfield—Lou "The Mad Russian" Novikoff
Outfield—Red Murray
Catcher—Red Dooin
Pitcher—Lefty Gomez

DON VITO CORLEONE

First base—Joe Pepitone
Second base—Tony Lazzeri
Third base—Joe Torre
Shortstop—Phil Rizzuto
Outfield—Joe DiMaggio
Outfield—Rocky Colavito
Outfield—Carl Furillo
Catcher—Yogi Berra
Pitcher—Sal Maglie

FRANK BUCK

First base—Snake Deal
Second base—Nellie Fox
Third base—Possum Whitted
Shortstop—Rabbit Maranville
Outfield—Mule Haas
Outfield—Goat Anderson
Outfield—Ox Eckhardt
Catcher—Doggie Miller
Pitcher—Old Hoss Radbourn

e.e. cummings

first base—r.c. stevens
second base—a.j. mccoy
third base—i.i. mathison
shortstop—j.c. hartman

outfield—g.g. walker
outfield—j.w. porter
outfield—r.e. hildebrand
catcher—j.c. martin
pitcher—w.a. kearns

GOLDA MEIR

First base—Ron Blomberg
Second base—Rod Carew
Third base—Al Rosen
Shortstop—Eddie Feinberg
Outfield—Hank Greenberg
Outfield—Cal Abrams
Outfield—Goody Rosen
Catcher—Joe Ginsberg
Pitcher—Sandy Koufax

GOV. ALFRED E. SMITH

First base—Willie Smith
Second base—George Smith
Third base—Charlie Smith
Shortstop—Billy Smith
Outfield—Al Smith
Outfield—Reggie Smith
Outfield—Elmer Smith
Catcher—Hal Smith
Pitcher—Al Smith

BETTY FRIEDAN

First base—Mary Calhoun
Second base—Sadie Houck
Third base—She Donahue
Shortstop—Lena Blackburne
Outfield—Gail Henley
Outfield—Baby Doll Jacobson

Outfield—Estel Crabtree
Catcher—Bubbles Hargrave
Pitcher—Lil Stoner

JAMES BEARD

First base—Juice Latham
Second base—Peaches Graham
Third base—Pie Traynor
Shortstop—Chico Salmon
Outfield—Soupy Campbell
Outfield—Oyster Burns
Outfield—Peanuts Lowery
Catcher—Pickles Dillhoefer
Pitcher—Noodles Hahn

J. P. MORGAN

First base—Norm Cash
Second base—Don Money
Third base—Milton Stock
Shortstop—Ernie Banks
Outfield—Art Ruble
Outfield—Elmer Pence
Outfield—Bobby Bonds
Catcher—Gene Green
Pitcher—Jim Grant

JOHN JAMES AUDUBON

First base—Andy Swan
Second base—Johnny Peacock
Third base—Jiggs Parrott
Shortstop—Chicken Stanley
Outfield—Ducky Medwick
Outfield—Goose Goslin
Outfield—Bill Eagle

Catcher—Birdie Tebbetts
Pitcher—Robin Roberts

FRANK FIELD

First base—Sunny Jim Bottomley
Second base—Nippy Jones
Third base—Gene Freese
Shortstop—Stormy Weatherly
Outfield—Hurricane Hazle
Outfield—Curt Flood
Outfield—Icicle Reeder
Catcher—Sun Daly
Pitcher—Windy McCall

JIMMY the GREEK

First base—Frank Chance
Second base—Lucky Jack Lohrke
Third base—Charlie Deal
Shortstop—John Gamble
Outfield—Curt Welch
Outfield—Trick McSorley
Outfield—Ace Parker
Catcher—Candy LaChance
Pitcher—Shufflin' Phil Douglas

NORMAN VINCENT PEALE

First base—Earl Grace
Second base—Johnny Priest
Third base—Frank Bishop
Shortstop—Angel Hermoso
Outfield—Dave Pope
Outfield—Hi Church
Outfield—Maurice Archdeacon
Catcher—Mickey Devine
Pitcher—Howie Nunn

FOSTER BROOKS

First base—Sherry Robertson
Second base—Mickey Finn
Third base—Billy Lush
Shortstop—Bobby Wine
Outfield—Jigger Statz
Outfield—Brandy Davis
Outfield—Half Pint Rye
Catcher—George Gibson
Pitcher—John Boozer

RAND-McNALLY

First base—Frank Brazill
Second base—Chile Gomez
Third base—Frenchy Bordagaray
Shortstop—Sal Madrid
Outfield—Germany Schaefer
Outfield—Dutch Holland
Outfield—Clyde Milan
Catcher—Dick West
Pitcher—Vinegar Bend Mizell

QUEEN ELIZABETH

First base—Duke Carmel
Second base—Royal Shaw
Third base—Count Campau
Shortstop—John Knight
Outfield—Prince Oana
Outfield—Bris Lord
Outfield—Mel Queen
Catcher—Earl Averill
Pitcher—Clyde King

4 Baseball-Playing Palindromes

A palindrome is a word, or name, that reads the same backwards and forwards. In the history of baseball, there have been only four major league players whose last names read the same backwards and forwards.

1. Truck HANNAH, New York Yankees, 1918–1920
2. Toby HARRAH, Washington Senators, 1971; Texas Rangers, 1972–
3. Eddie KAZAK, St. Louis Cardinals, 1948–1952; Cincinnati Reds, 1952
4. Dick NEN, Los Angeles Dodgers, 1963; Washington Senators, 1965–1967; Chicago Cubs, 1968

26 Famous Baseball Batteries Made Up of Pitchers and Catchers Who, Unfortunately, Never Played Together, But Did, in Fact, Play in the Major Leagues and Only Chance Prevented Us from Hearing the Public Address Announcer Say, "The Battery for Today's Game . . ."

1. East and West
2. Johnson and Johnson
3. Holly and Ivie
4. Barnes and Noble
5. Hand and Foote
6. Burns and Allen
7. Black and White
8. Butcher and Baker
9. Nixon and Agnew
10. Kennedy and Johnson
11. Lewis and Clark

Willard Nixon of the Boston
Red Sox.   *UPI*

Sam Agnew of the St. Louis
Browns.   *UPI*

12. Rogers and Hart
13. Gilbert and Sullivan
14. Franklin and Marshall
15. Hale and Hardy
16. Bell and Howell
17. Mason and Dixon
18. Masters and Johnson
19. Black and Decker
20. More and Moore
21. Blue and Grey
22. Queen and King
23. High and Lowe
24. Reid and Wright
25. Short and Long
26. Stanley and Livingston

Real Names of 37 Well-Known Baseball Players

1. Ping Bodie   (Francesco Stephano Pezzolo)
2. Sammy Bohne   (Samuel Arthur Cohen)
3. Bunny Brief   (Antonio Bordetzki)
4. Andy Carey   (Andrew Arthur Nordstrom)
5. Max Carey   (Maximillian Carnarius)
6. Joe Collins   (Joseph Edward Kollonige)
7. Stan Coveleski   (Stanislaus Kowalewski)
8. Frank Demaree   (Joseph Franklin DiMaria)
9. Johnny Dickshot   (John Arthur Dicksus)
10. Cozy Dolan   (James Alberts)
11. Mickey Doolan   (Michael Joseph Doolittle)
12. Joe Glenn   (Joseph Charles Gurzensky)
13. Pete Gray   (Peter J. Wyshner)
14. Eddie Kazak   (Edward Terrence Tkaczuk)
15. Dick Kokos   (Richard Jerome Kokoszka)
16. Joe Koppe   (Joseph Kopchia)
17. Dave Koslo   (George Bernard Koslowski)
18. Sandy Koufax   (Sanford Braun)
19. Ed Levy   (Edward Clarence Whitner)
20. Eddie Lopat   (Edmund Walter Lopatyaski)
21. Connie Mack   (Cornelius Alexander McGillicuddy)
22. Ray Mack   (Raymond James Mlckovsky)
23. Lee Magee   (Leopold Christopher Hoernschmeyer)
24. Duke Markell   (Harry Duquesne Marowsky)
25. Babe Martin   (Boris Michael Martinovich)
26. Billy Martin   (Alfred Manuel Pesano)
27. Eddie Mayo   (Edward Joseph Mayoski)
28. Charlie Metro   (Charles Moreskonich)
29. Cass Michaels   (Casimir Eugene Kwietniewski)
30. Erv Palica   (Ervin Walter Pavliecivich)

31. Johnny Pesky	(John Michael Paveskovich)
32. Tony Piet	(Anthony Francis Pietruska)
33. Babe Pinelli	(Rinaldo Angelo Paolinelli)
34. Jimmy Reese	(James Hymie Soloman)
35. Al Simmons	(Aloysius Harry Szymanski)
36. Hal Trosky	(Harold Arthur Troyavesky)
37. Whitey Witt	(Ladislaw Waldemar Wittkowski)

Ray Robinson's All-Time Middle-Name Baseball Team

Ray Robinson, whose own middle name is Kenneth, is a journalist, book author, and magazine editor (*Real, Pageant, Coronet, Good Housekeeping, Seventeen*), with a special passion for baseball miscellany. Several of his baseball articles have been anthologized in *The Fireside Book of Baseball* and *Best Sports Stories of the Year*. He lists the Bobo Newsom Chowder and Marching Society as his chief club affiliation.

"Only once have I been called upon to use my middle name," he says. "Many years ago I sold a boxing fiction piece to *Collier's*. The editors feared the readers might confuse me with a slightly better welterweight named Sugar Ray Robinson, so I was forced to insert my middle name into the byline. I've been obsessed with middle names ever since."

First base—Jack ROOSEVELT Robinson
Second base—Robert PERSHING Doerr
Shortstop—Mark ANTHONY Koenig
Third base—Robert ABIAL Rolfe
Right field—George HERMAN Ruth
Center field—Tyrus RAYMOND Cobb

Jack Roosevelt Robinson's middle name derived from another Rough Rider, President Theodore Roosevelt.

UPI

Left field—Floyd CAVES Herman
Catcher—William McKINLEY Hargrave
Pitcher—Robert MOSES Grove
Pitcher—Van LINGLE Mungo
Pitcher—George LIVINGSTON Earnshaw
Pitcher—Denton TECUMSEH Young
Pitcher—Jay HANNER (or HANNA) Dean or
        Jerome HERMAN Dean
Pitcher—Daniel KNOWLES MacFayden
Hitting Coach—Paul GLEE Waner
Manager—Charles DILLON Stengel
Baseball Writer—Daniel M. Daniel
Commissioner—Kenesaw MOUNTAIN Landis
Fixer—Joseph JEFFERSON Jackson

Robinson notes: Most romantic pick has to be Mark Anthony Koenig . . . . George Herman Ruth owns the three best-known names in baseball history . . . . Most appropriate middle name is Paul Waner's "Glee"; he was the man who delighted in one too many, and I don't mean base hits . . . . The M in Daniel Daniel breaks up the monotony . . . . George Livingston Earnshaw is by far the most patrician array of names in sports history . . . . Cobb's nondescript middle name belongs only because it's my first name . . . . Take your choice of Dean middle names and also flip a coin for his home state—Arkansas, Oklahoma, Texas . . . . Daniel Knowles MacFayden was, in truth, a best-selling author . . . . And F. Caves Herman was as much a shining beacon of the Roaring Twenties as F. Scott Fitzgerald.

12 Athletes Better Known by "Whitey" Than Their Real First Names

1. Whitey Ford   (Edward Charles)
2. Whitey Kurowski   (George John)

 3. Whitey Bimstein   (Morris)
 4. Whitey Witt   (Lawton Walker)
 5. Whitey Skoog   (Meyer)
 6. Whitey Wietelmann   (William Frederick)
 7. Whitey Lockman   (Carroll Walter)
 8. Whitey Bell   (William)
 9. Whitey Herzog   (Dorrel Norman Elvert)
10. Whitey Martin   (Ronald)
11. Whitey Stapleton   (Patrick James)
12. Whitey Widing   (Juha Marrku)

Bill Madden's Most Valuable Sports Autographs

Formerly with United Press International, now with the *New York News*, Bill Madden is an inveterate collector of sports memorabilia. He writes a column on the subject of collecting for the *Sporting News*.

He explains: Autographs, like all sports collectibles, can be divided into two categories when it comes to value: baseball and nonbaseball. Because of the game's lore and the mystique surrounding its heroes of the past, baseball items are in a class by themselves among collectors. Therefore, when it comes to autographs, the most sought-after and valued are those of baseball players. However, their value depends upon what the autographs are written on. Autographed baseballs, for example, are worth more than autographed pictures, but an autographed picture has a higher value than a simple piece of paper with an autograph.

1. Pre-1900 Hall of Fame players—For example, John Clarkson, Mickey Welch, Pud Galvin, Harry Wright. Naturally, baseball Hall of Famers are more valued than other players, but to the true collector that value is not necessarily determined by the player's greatness.

Rather, it is the least attainable autographs that capture the true collector's fancy. In the case of old-timers like Galvin, Clarkson, and others, only one or two autographs are known to exist. Many of these can be found on old letters and other forms of correspondence between these players and their families, or on old contracts from the turn-of-the-century National League clubs.

2. Combination baseballs of Hall of Famers or historical baseball events—These are very popular items and they enable collectors to be creative in their selections. For example: .400 hitters, Hornsby, Cobb, Williams, etc.; Famous batteries, such as Larsen-Berra; Famous teammates, such as Ruth-Gehrig, Mantle-Maris.

3. Hall of Famers who died prematurely—As morbid as it may sound, a man's autograph only attains value upon his death. Thus, those Hall of Famers who died prematurely had less opportunity to sign autographs in their lifetimes. Lou Gehrig, Addie Joss, Christy Mathewson, and Rube Waddell fall in this category.

4. Deceased Negro League Hall of Famers and stars —With the recognition of the Negro Leagues by the baseball hierarchy, these stars have now gained new stature among collectors. Thus, a Josh Gibson and an Oscar Charleston, both deceased, are considered quite valuable since they, too, are not easily attained.

5. Nonplaying deceased executives—Alexander Cartwright, Ban Johnson, Morgan Bulkeley, all of whom served before or just after the turn of the century as baseball pioneers, are in this category. Naturally, this trio is among the hardest of Hall of Fame autographs to attain. Abner Doubleday is one of the most sought-after autographs, but not among baseball purists, who know he never had anything to do with the game of baseball and is, consequently, omitted from the Hall of Fame.

6. Team baseballs—Autographed team balls are always a very popular collector's item, especially among new collectors. All of today's teams make their autograph team balls available to the public for sale at the ballpark. However, the really valuable autographed baseballs are of those teams prior to 1925, which are nearly nonexistent. In addition, such teams as the Yankees of the late '30s (which had both Gehrig and DiMaggio) or those rare teams such as the 1944 St. Louis Browns or 1950 Philadelphia Phillies, which won only once, are also much sought-after. Probably the most valuable team ball of all, however, is that of the most famous team of all, the 1927 New York Yankees' Murderer's Row. With six Hall of Famers, including Ruth and Gehrig, this ball could command as much as $500 in good shape.

7. Stars who, for one reason or another, refuse to sign autographs or have done so very infrequently—This is the only category in which live players' autographs can be valuable, again because they are unattainable. Some players noted for being stingy with their autographs are Mike Marshall, Bob Gibson, Pete Gray, Vada Pinson, and a rare nonbaseballer, basketball star Bill Russell. In the case of Marshall and Russell, both feel their autographs should not be something little kids value. No one knows why Gibson wouldn't sign, or Pinson, either. As for Gray, the theory is that he was sensitive to people wanting his autograph just because he had only one arm.

30 Sports Personalities Better Known by "Red" Than Their Real First Names

1. Red Rolfe   (Robert Abial)
2. Red Grange   (Harold)

3.	Red Holzman	(William)
4.	Red Ruffing	(Charles Herbert)
5.	Red Barber	(Walter Lanier)
6.	Red Kress	(Ralph)
7.	Red Sullivan	(George James)
8.	Red Sarachek	(Bernard)
9.	Red Lucas	(Charles Fred)
10.	Red Killefer	(Wade)
11.	Red Jones	(Maurice Morris)
12.	Red Auerbach	(Arnold)
13.	Red Cochrane	(Freddie)
14.	Red Wolfe	(George)
15.	Red Sanders	(Henry)
16.	Red Schoendienst	(Albert Fred)
17.	Red Hayworth	(Myron Claude)
18.	Red Miller	(Robert)
19.	Red Burman	(Clarence)
20.	Red Faber	(Urban Clarence)
21.	Red Smith	(Walter Wellesley)
22.	Red Berenson	(Gordon)
23.	Red Blaik	(Earl)
24.	Red Murff	(John Robert)
25.	Red Kelly	(Leonard Patrick)
26.	Red Mack	(William)
27.	Red Munger	(George David)
28.	Red Barrett	(Charles Henry)
29.	Red Embree	(Charles Willard)
30.	Red Rocha	(Ephraim)

Real Names of 33 Well-Known Fighters

Ring name	(Real Name)
1. Lou Ambers	(Louis D'Amrobsio)
2. Henry Armstrong	(Henry Jackson)

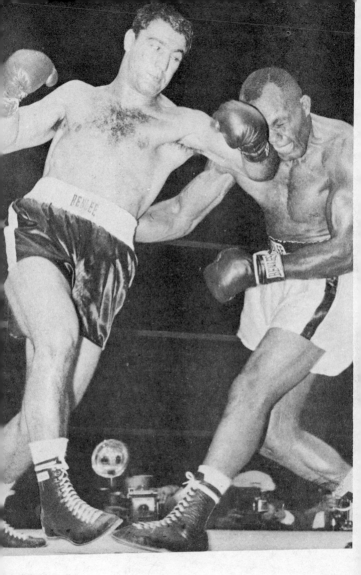

En route to his heavyweight championship, Rocco Marchegiano lands a hard one on Jersey Joe Walcott. *UPI*

3. Jack Britton   (William Breslin)
4. Tommy Burns   (Noah Brusso)
5. Kid Chocolate   (Eligio Sardinias)
6. Jack Delaney   (Ovila Chapdelaine)
7. Jack Dempsey   (William Harrison Demp-
                            sey)

8. Jackie Fields   (Jacob Finkelstein)
9. Kid Gavilan   (Gerardo Gonzalez)
10. Rocky Graziano   (Rocco Barbella)
11. Beau Jack   (Sidney Walker)
12. Ben Jeby   (Morris Jebaltowski)
13. Lew Jenkins   (Verlin Jenks)
14. Stanley Ketchel   (Stanislaus Kiecal)
15. Tippy Larkin   (Anthony Pilleteri)
16. Benny Leonard   (Benjamin Leiner)
17. Joe Louis   (Joseph Louis Barrow)
18. Rocky Marciano   (Rocco Marchegiano)
19. Joey Maxim   (Giuseppe Antonio Berar-
                            dinelli)

20. Philadelphia Jack O'Brien   (Joseph Hagen)
21. Packey O'Gatty   (Pasquale Agati)
22. Lee Oma   (Frank Czjewski)
23. Young Otto   (Arthur Susskind)
24. Willie Pep   (William Papaleo)
25. Sugar Ray Robinson   (Walker Smith)
26. Barney Ross   (Barnet David Rasofsky)
27. Jack Sharkey   (Joseph Paul Cukoschay)
28. Battling Siki   (Louis Phal)
29. Pancho Villa   (Francisco Guilledo)
30. Jersey Joe Walcott   (Arnold Raymond Cream)
31. Midget Wolgast   (Joseph Loscatzo)
32. Tony Zale   (Anthony Florian Zaleski)
33. Zulu Kid   (Joseph Dimelfi)

SOURCE: *The Ring Boxing Encyclopedia and Record Book* (The Ring
Book Shop).

40 Indians (Not Washington Redskins) Who Played Professional Football

In 1922, the legendary Jim Thorpe, an Indian out of Carlisle College, organized a team called the Oorang Indians, which played for Marion (Ohio) in the National Football League. The team disbanded after 2–6 and 1–10 records, but others of Indian blood have played pro football.

1. Arrowhead, end, Oorang Indians
2. Barrel, center, Oorang Indians
3. Big Bear, tackle, Oorang Indians
4. Big Twig, guard, Buffalo Bisons
5. Black Bear, end, Oorang Indians
6. Leon Boutwell, quarterback, Oorang Indians
7. Buffalo, guard, Oorang Indians
8. Elmer Busch, guard, Oorang Indians
9. Pete Calac, end, Cleveland Indians, Canton Bulldogs, Oorang Indians, Buffalo Bisons
10. Deadeye, tackle, Oorang Indians
11. Deerslayer, end, Oorang Indians
12. Eagle Feather, back, Oorang Indians
13. Albert Exendine, Massillon
14. Gray Horse, back, Oorang Indians
15. Joe Guyon, back, Cleveland Indians, Oorang Indians, Rock Island Indians, Kansas City Cowboys, New York Giants
16. Long Tim Sleep (Nick Lassa), center, Oorang Indians
17. Laughing Gas, back, Oorang Indians
18. Little Boy, back, Columbus Panhandles
19. Little Twig, tackle, Oorang Indians, Rock Island Independents
20. Lone Star, tackle, Columbus Panhandles

21. Lone Wolf, guard, Oorang Indians
22. Frank Mt. Pleasant, Massillon
23. Newashe, tackle, Oorang Indians
24. Bemus Pierce, Massillon
25. Hawey Pierce, Massillon
26. Jim Plunkett, quarterback, New England Patriots, San Francisco 49ers, Oakland Raiders
27. Stancil Powell, guard, Oorang Indians
28. Red Fang, tackle, Oorang Indians
29. Red Foot, end, Oorang Indians
30. Red Fox, back, Oorang Indians
31. Running Deer, end, Oorang Indians
32. Theodore St. Germain, guard, Oorang Indians
33. Saunook, end, Oorang Indians
34. Seeds, back, Canton Bulldogs
35. Jack Thorpe, guard, Oorang Indians
36. Jim Thorpe, back, Cleveland Indians, Canton Bulldogs, Oorang Indians, Rock Island Independents, New York Giants
37. Tomahawk, back, Oorang Indians
38. Towell, back, Oorang Indians
39. Welmus Woodchuck, end, Oorang Indians
40. Wrinkle Meat, guard, Oorang Indians

50 Unlikeliest Names for the Mammoth Crushers of Pro Football

1. Adrian Baril
2. Kay Bell
3. Lynn Bomar
4. Marion Broadstone
5. Gail Bruce

After Carlisle College, Jim Thorpe achieved fame in the Olympics, and in pro football and major league baseball.   *UPI*

6. Adrian Burk
7. Lynn Chandnois
8. Pearl Clarke
9. Gail Clarke
10. Bree Cupolette
11. Carroll Dale
12. Marion Dirks
13. Leslie Duncan
14. Kay Eakin
15. Robin Earl
16. Adrian Ford
17. Leslie Grace
18. Kim Hammond
19. Carroll Hardy
20. Fair Hooker
21. Leslie Horvath
22. Lynn Hoyem
23. Allison Hubert
24. Vivian Huhman
25. June Jones
26. Kim Jones
27. Shelby Jordan
28. Kerry Justin
29. Emerald Lamme
30. Leslie Lane
31. Leslie Lear
32. Lynn Lynch
33. Blanche Martin
34. Marion Motley
35. Laurie Niemi
36. Gail O'Brien
37. Marion Pugh
38. Clair Purdy
39. Carroll Raborn
40. Clare Randolph

41. Carroll Ringwalt
42. Kyle Rote
43. Goldie Sellers
44. Marion Shirley
45. Leslie Shy
46. Lynn Swann
47. Vivian Vanderloo
48. Laurie Walquist
49. Faye Wilson
50. Carroll Zaruba

V

---

3 Yards and a Cloud of Dust

Johnny Unitas' Super Bowl All-Star Team

OFFENSE

Wide Receiver—Lynn Swann, Pittsburgh Steelers
Wide Receiver—Max McGee, Green Bay Packers
Wide Receiver—Fred Biletnikoff, Oakland Raiders
Tight End—Dave Casper, Oakland Raiders
Tackle—Forrest Gregg, Green Bay Packers
Tackle—Ralph Neely, Dallas Cowboys
Guard—Fred Thurston, Green Bay Packers
Guard—Gene Upshaw, Oakland Raiders
Center—Jim Otto, Oakland Raiders
Quarterback—Bart Starr, Green Bay Packers
Half back—Clarence Davis, Oakland Raiders
Full back—Franco Harris, Pittsburgh Steelers

Johnny Unitas' starting quarterback: Green Bay's Bart Starr.

Malcolm Emmons

DEFENSE

End—L.C. Greenwood, Pittsburgh Steelers
End—Harvey Martin, Dallas Cowboys
Tackle—Bob Lilly, Dallas Cowboys
Tackle—Joe Greene, Pittsburgh Steelers
Outside Linebacker—Mike Curtis, Baltimore Colts
Outside Linebacker—Jack Ham, Pittsburgh Steelers
Middle Linebacker—Jack Lambert, Pittsburgh Steelers
Corner back—Herb Adderly, Green Bay Packers
Corner back—Mel Blount, Pittsburgh Steelers
Safety—Willie Wood, Green Bay Packers
Safety—Jack Scott, Miami Dolphins

SPECIALISTS

Punter—Jerrel Wilson, Kansas City Chiefs
Place Kicker—Jan Stenerud, Kansas City Chiefs
Kick Returner—Mike Garrett, Kansas City Chiefs

COACH

Vince Lombardi, Green Bay Packers

SOURCE: *The Complete Handbook of Pro Football* (NAL Signet).

Curt Gowdy's All-Time Pro Team

OFFENSE

Quarterback—Joe Namath
Running Backs—O.J. Simpson
                     Larry Csonka
Wide Receivers—Paul Warfield
                     Lance Alworth

O.J. Simpson made Curt Gowdy's team.

Jerry Wachter

Center—Jim Otto
Guards—Jerry Kramer
            Billy Shaw
Tackles—Rayfield Wright
            Ron Yary
Tight End—John Mackey
Place Kickers—Jan Stenerud
                    George Blanda

DEFENSE

Ends—Rich "Tombstone" Jackson
        Deacon Jones
Tackles—Bob Lilly
            Joe Greene
Linebackers—Dick Butkus
                    Dave Robinson
                    Bobby Bell
Corner Backs—Willie Brown
                    Herb Adderly
Safeties—Dick Anderson
            Johnny Robinson
Punter—Ray Guy
Coach—Don Shula

SOURCE: *The Complete Handbook of Pro Football* (NAL Signet).

Lindsey Nelson's 10 Most Memorable Football Games

Lindsey Nelson is one of the most respected sports broadcasters of all time. Literate, personable, and articulate, he has been broadcasting for more than three decades, during which time he has witnessed almost every major football Bowl game. With Bob Murphy and Ralph Kiner, Nelson was the voice of the New York Mets from their inception in 1962 through 1978. His list is of games he has broadcast.

(Above) It's the Cotton Bowl, Alabama vs. Rice, 1954, and No. 42 on the sidelines, Tommy Lewis, watches Rice's Dicky Moegle (white shirt) running with the ball. (Below) Moegle about to be tackled by Lewis, who had leaped onto the field and surprised Moegle and everyone else. Referee Cliff Shaw awarded Moegle a touchdown. Rice won. 28-6.   *UPI*

1. Alabama vs. Rice, Cotton Bowl, 1954—"Tommy Lewis came off the bench to tackle Rice's Dickie Moegle 'on camera.' The Alabama quarterback was Bart Starr."

2. Montreal Alouettes vs. Edmonton Eskimoes, Grey Cup, 1954—"Jackie Parker of Edmonton returned a Montreal fumble the length of the field to beat a Montreal team that starred Sam Etchevarry, Hal Patterson, Tex Coulter, and Alex Webster."

3. Baltimore Colts vs. Detroit Lions, Baltimore, 1960—"Johnny Unitas hit Lenny Moore with a TD pass with 11 seconds to play to put Baltimore ahead, but Detroit came back to win on a TD pass to Jim Gibbons."

4. Utah vs. Brigham Young, Salt Lake City, Thanksgiving Day, 1953—"Utah, coached by Jack Curtice, won 32-31."

5. Syracuse vs. TCU, Cotton Bowl, 1957—"Jim Brown vs. Jim Swink. TCU won, 28-27."

6. Philadelphia Eagles vs. Green Bay Packers, Franklin Field, Philadelphia, NFL Championship Game, 1960—"Vince Lombardi's first title game and he lost to Buck Shaw. It was Norm Van Brocklin's last game. Packer stars were Bart Starr, Paul Hornung, Jim Taylor. Eagle stars were Van Brocklin, Tommy McDonald, Tom Brookshier."

7. Tennessee vs. Kentucky, Knoxville, Tenn., 1950—"Coaches: Gen. Bob Neyland vs. Paul "Bear" Bryant. Hank Lauricella vs. Babe Parilli. Tennessee won, 7-0, in the snow."

8. Notre Dame vs. Texas, Cotton Bowl, 1972—"The second meeting of these two teams in the Cotton Bowl. Notre Dame used the 'Mirror Defense' to stop the Texas 'Wishbone' and the Irish won the game."

9. Michigan State vs. UCLA, Rose Bowl, 1966—"UCLA, quarterbacked by Gary Beban and coached by Tommy

Prothro, upset a Michigan team coached by Duffy Daugherty and starring Bubba Smith."

10. Notre Dame vs. Southern California, 1977—"Notre Dame, which used normal blue jerseys in pre-game drills, switched to green for the game and rolled to a decisive victory behind Joe Montana and Ken McAfee and on to the national championship."

Woody Hayes' 6 Greatest Victories

It was hard to miss Wayne Woodrow Hayes on the Ohio State sidelines. For nearly 30 years the stubby man with glasses, gray hair, and baseball cap dictatorially guided the Ohio State football team. In that time, the Buckeyes were national champions three times (1954 No. 1 by AP, 1957 No. 1 by UPI, 1968 consensus No. 1) and Rose Bowl champions four times (1955, 1958, 1969, 1974).

1. Ohio State 21, Michigan 7, Nov. 20, 1954—A 99⅔-yard drive to a touchdown after the Buckeye defense stopped Michigan on the goal line gave Ohio State only its fourth victory over the Wolverines in 17 years. It also made the alumni tear down the "Goodbye Woody" signs.

2. Ohio State 20, Southern California 7, Jan. 1, 1955— What better way to cap the 1954 season than a Rose Bowl victory and a No. 1 ranking by AP? Woody had given Ohio State its first undefeated season in 10 years.

3. Ohio State 13, Purdue 0, Oct. 12, 1968—Woody said his crop of sophomores was the best ever at Ohio State. After two victories came unbeaten Purdue, big, tough, and fast. But as Woody said afterwards, "It's never an upset if the so-called underdog has all along considered itself the better team."

4. Ohio State 27, Southern California 16, Jan. 1, 1969—

A running back named O.J. Simpson meant nothing to Woody's unbeaten super sophs. Playing for the national championship against Southern Cal in the Rose Bowl, the young Buckeyes rallied from a 10-0 deficit to win, scoring twice off Southern Cal fumbles. AP later voted this Buckeye squad the team of the decade.

5. Ohio State 20, Michigan 9, Nov. 21, 1970—Woody put a rug outside the locker room that read: "1969: Michigan 24, Ohio State 12. 1970: ?" Before the game he received a telegram: "This one literally is for a lifetime." Michigan had no chance against a team about which one reporter said, "Those guys aren't sane."

6. Ohio State 42, Southern California 21, Jan. 1, 1974— Woody had been crushed, 42-17, by Southern Cal in the 1973 Rose Bowl. But Archie Griffin and Company made sure Woody got what he wanted—revenge.

SOURCE: *Woody Hayes and the 100-Yard War* by Jerry Brondfield (Random House).

Herman Masin's 10 Greatest High School Quarterbacks, from 1951 to 1978

Herman L. Masin is editor of *Scholastic Coach,* which annually selects High School All-America teams in football, basketball, and track and field.

1. Bart Starr, Lanier High School, Montgomery, Ala., 1951
2. Fran Tarkenton, Athens High School, Athens, Ga., 1956
3. Joe Namath, Beaver Falls High School, Beaver Falls, Pa., 1960
4. Sonny Jurgensen, Wilmington High School, Wilmington, N.C., 1952

5. Ken Stabler, Foley High School, Foley, Ala., 1963
6. Bob Griese, Rex Mundi High School, Evansville, Ind., 1962
7. Earl Morrall, Muskegon High School, Muskegon, Mich., 1951
8. Len Dawson, Alliance High School, Alliance, Ohio, 1952
9. Daryle Lamonica, Clovis High School, Clovis, Cal., 1958
10. Roman Gabriel, Wilmington High School, Wilmington, N.C., 1957

Says Masin: "All in all, we have chosen about 30 QBs who went on to achieve fame in college and the pros. Five won the Heisman Trophy. About 20 made it to the pros.

"The unique point about the High School All-America is that it is incredibly tough to pick offensive and defensive linemen, virtually impossible to pick defensive backs, hard to pick ends, difficult, but possible, to pick running backs. But QBs? Duck soup. (At least for us.) The kid who stands out in high school is the kid who goes on to make it big later on. This isn't true in any other position. (In basketball, it's true about 90 percent of the time.)

"The above list is the elite. Since it was patently absurd to evaluate the players off their high school records (if that were the case we would have heroic names like Jack Norwood and John Maio on the list ahead of Bart Starr and Joe Namath), we chose as our guideline the eventual success achieved by the player. Greatness in every athlete is always measured by how well the player does in the pros. That has to be the final crucible. Did the player stand up to the toughest competition of all? And so we had to discard great High School and College All-Americas such as John Huarte, George Izo, Terry Hanratty, and at least two dozen other kids with staggering stats.

"If I may, I would like to add a 'Watch Out For' list:

"1. Richard Todd, Davidson High School, Davidson, Ala., 1971.

"2. Pat Haden, Bishop Amat High School, LaPuente, Cal., 1970.

"3. Steve Bartkowski, Buchser High School, Santa Clara, Cal., 1970.

"I add this 'Watch Out For' list for one obvious reason: All our All-Americas from 1970 on haven't had a real chance to prove themselves yet."

Dave Nelson's 21 Most Important Rules Changes in College Football History

Dave Nelson was a star football player at Michigan and, for 15 years, a successful head coach at the University of Delaware, where he is director of athletics. He has been the editor and secretary of the Football Rules Committee of the NCAA since 1961 and is the author of several books on football.

1. Scrimmage established replacing the scrum, 1880
2. Players reduced from 15 to 11, 1880
3. Touchdown changed to player possession on or over the goal line, 1900
4. Forward pass enters the game, 1906
5. Actual playing time, 60 minutes, 1906
6. Seven offensive players required on line of scrimmage, 1910
7. First player receiving snap may advance the ball beyond the neutral zone, 1910
8. Three downs and five yards for a first down changed to four downs and 10 yards, 1912
9. End zones established, 1912
10. Football code added to rules, 1916
11. Huddle added to the rules, 1916

12. Scrimmage kick behind neutral zone advanced by either team, 1925
13. Size of ball reduced to increase passing, 1926
14. Hash marks at 10 yards, 1933
15. All players must wear head protectors, 1939
16. Two platoon football possible, 1941
17. Forward pass legal anywhere behind the neutral zone. Five-yard restriction eliminated, 1945
18. Face masks made legal, 1951
19. One platoon football returns, 1953
20. Two-point conversion, 1958
21. Goal posts widened from 18 feet, 5 inches, to 23 feet, 4 inches, 1959

ABC's Wide World of Sports Special

Lew Alcindor's Pro Debut

MILWAUKEE VS DETROIT

Live
2:00PM

abc **Saturday** 7

ABC-TV

VI

Hoops

Basketball's 13 Greatest Games

1. Milwaukee Bucks vs. Detroit Pistons, October 18, 1969—ABC-TV juggled its schedule to bring the nation's sports fans the professional debut of Lew Alcindor (Kareem Abdul-Jabbar), the three-time All-America from UCLA. A crowd of 7,782 in Milwaukee Arena watched the new Buck jump off against the Pistons. For those who doubted his ability to play in the pros, Alcindor provided these answers in the Bucks' 119-110 victory—29 points, 12 rebounds, six assists, three blocked shots, three pass interceptions.
2. Michigan vs. Princeton, December, 1964—Michigan's Cazzie Russell vs. Princeton's Bill Bradley, a classic in old Madison Square Garden. The brawny, shot-happy Cazzie against brainy, team-playing Bradley. And this Holiday Festival semifinal was no disappointment. Bradley's 23 first-half points put Ivy League Princeton in front, 39-37. With four minutes to play, underdog

Princeton's Bill Bradley drives past Michigan's Cazzie Russell. *UPI*

Princeton built a 13-point lead on the strength of 41 points from Bradley. But when Bradley fouled out, Russell went to work, scoring 11 points to lead Michigan to an 80-78 come-from-behind victory.

3. Los Angeles Lakers vs. Philadelphia Warriors, December 8, 1961—The fans in Philadelphia's Convention Center were in for quite a night. It was the Lakers, with Elgin Baylor and Jerry West, against the Warriors and Wilt Chamberlain. By halftime, a scoring duel was in progress: Wilt had scored 28 points, Elgin 16. Going into the final period, it was Chamberlain 38 points, Baylor 32. After regulation time, Wilt had 53 points, Elgin 47. After one overtime, it was Wilt over Elgin, 62-50. And going into the third overtime, Chamberlain led, 68-59. When the game ended, Chamberlain had scored 78 points to break Baylor's NBA record of 73. Wilt also set single-game records for shots taken (62) and field goals made (31). Baylor had scored 63 points, but his Lakers were on the long end of a 151-147 score.

4. New York Knicks vs. Los Angeles Lakers, 1970 NBA Championship Final Series, Game 5—The series was tied, 2-2, and early in the first period, the Knicks' center and captain, Willis Reed, was hurt and had to leave the game. Outmanned, the Knicks fell behind after three periods, 82-75, to a team that included Wilt Chamberlain, Jerry West, and Elgin Baylor. But the New Yorkers staged a valiant comeback to win, 107-100, without their injured star, to whom they dedicated the victory.

5. Seattle U. vs. Harlem Globetrotters, January 21, 1952 —Johnny O'Brien, one half of Seattle's twin brother act, scored 43 points as the Chieftains beat the famous

Globetrotters, 84–81, in a game played for the benefit of the United States Olympic Committee.

6. Philadelphia Warriors vs. New York Knicks, March 2, 1962—Wilt Chamberlain bombed the Knicks for an amazing 100 points in Hershey, Pa., shattering the league single game scoring record. The Big Dipper also set other records: most field goals attempted (63), most field goals made (36), and most free throws made (28).

7. Niagara vs. Siena, February 21, 1953, Washington Avenue Armory, Albany, N.Y.—Niagara, led by future NBA coaches Larry Costello and Hubie Brown, was regarded as one of the best teams in the East. Siena was rated no better than a good small college team. But they battled through five overtimes, the game starting at 9:15 p.m. and ending at 12:17 a.m., before Niagara sealed an 88–81 victory in the longest game ever played. Costello played 70 minutes, the most ever played in a single game.

8. Houston vs. UCLA, January 20, 1968—A record crowd of 52,693 showed up in the Houston Astrodome for the super game. UCLA, led by Lew Alcindor (Kareem Abdul-Jabbar), hadn't lost in two years. Houston, starring Elvin Hayes, was unbeaten since a loss to UCLA the previous season. But supported by a partisan, home-town crowd, Houston scored a 71–69 upset as Hayes outscored Alcindor, 39–15.

9. East-West College All-Star Game, Madison Square Garden, March 30, 1946—It was the first East-West game ever, the West led by giants Bob Kurland and Don Otten, augmented by a sprinkling of players returned from World War II. The East featured Harry Boykoff and Sid Tannenbaum, but a 17-year-old Colgate freshman, Ernie Vandeweghe, stole the show,

scoring 14 points and setting up four important baskets in the last half, including the game winner, to give the East a 60-59 victory. For his efforts, Vandeweghe was voted MVP of the game.

10. Boston Celtics vs. Syracuse Nationals, Boston Garden, March 21, 1953—It was the second game of the NBA's Eastern Division playoffs. Bob Cousy was his magical self throughout the game, scoring 25 points that included a free throw to tie the game with five seconds remaining. In the four overtimes that followed, Cousy was spectacular. He tied the game three times in the final seconds, the last with a desperate half-court shot at the buzzer. He scored nine points in the fourth overtime as the Celtics scored a 111-105 victory. Cousy scored 50 points for the game, half of them in overtime.

11. Kansas U. vs. North Carolina, Kansas Municipal Auditorium, March 23, 1957—Led by the invincible giant, Wilt Chamberlain, Kansas figured to have little trouble with North Carolina's rebels from the sidewalks of New York in this NCAA final. But they battled through three overtimes, the first in NCAA final history, until Brooklynite Joe Quigg sank a pair of free throws with six seconds left in the third OT to give the "North" Carolinians a 54-53 victory as the Tar Heels finished 32-0.

12. Boston Celtics vs. Phoenix Suns, Boston Garden, Game 5 of the 1976 NBA Final Championship Series —With the series tied, 2-2, the Celtics and Suns met in late May in one of the most exciting playoff games in NBA history. They went three overtimes, one of the longest games on record. The Suns might have won had the referee not ignored a time out call of Celtic

A crowd of 52,693 at the Houston Astrodome saw Houston (Elvin Hayes) snap UCLA's (Lew Alcindor) 47-game winning streak.   *UPI*

Paul Silas and the resulting technical foul call. The Celtics capitalized on the break, won the game, 128–126, and clinched the title two days later in Phoenix.

13. UCLA vs. North Carolina State, 1974 NCAA semi-finals—UCLA was back for its seventh title defense, led by the great Bill Walton. North Carolina State, with David Thompson, had lost to the Bruins by 18 points earlier in the season. Early in the game, UCLA jumped out to an 11-point lead. But the Wolfpack fought back to tie, 65-all, on a basket by Thompson. Again UCLA grabbed the lead, by seven, and again Thompson brought NC State back, his bank shot with 54 seconds left in overtime giving State a 76–75 lead. The Pack won the game, 80–77, then went on to defeat Marquette in the final game for the NCAA crown.

Leonard Koppett's 9 Rules Changes for Keeping the Score Down in Basketball

Leonard Koppett, formerly of The *New York Times*, has been a long-time analyst and critic of the sporting scene. He has written several books on basketball.

1. Attach the hoop to a revolving rod so that the hoop rotates through 360 degrees, slowly, making two revolutions every 24 seconds. Sometimes the plane of the hoop will be parallel to the floor, as it is now, sometimes it will be vertical, and most of the time it will be facing left or right. In this case, not only must each shot be aimed differently, but each rebound will come off at a different angle, giving the quick, clever man the advantage over the merely tall, strong man.

2. A variation of the above: Keep the basket-hoop steady, but move the whole backboard along a track, parallel to

the end line, from one side of the court to the other
—maybe at a steady rate, maybe at variable speeds.

3. The penalty for a personal foul shall be that the man
who makes it is forbidden to shoot at the basket for the
next minute (or two minutes, or 30 seconds). Most
players would rather die than face that restriction.

4. Raise the basket (but that would put the little man farther away).

5. Lower the basket (so everyone can throw the ball down
instead of up).

6. Put a lid on the basket with a pull-rope to open it.
Before you can score, a teammate has to get to the rope
and pull the basket open.

7. Bring back the net now that fine-spun nylon is available
and play the game in a cage again, so that the ball can
never be out of bounds; but make the top of the cage
only 6½ feet high.

8. Paint concentric semi-circles on the floor around the
basket. For each inch in height, a player must shoot
from one foot farther out, giving the shortest player in
the game no limitation (that is, he can shoot from
"zero" range).

9. On a blocking-charging collision, forget altogether
about determining who had legal floor position or right
of way. Instead, have a panel of judges at courtside—as
is done in judging figure skating competition—who will
hold up cards awarding points for the quality of acting
on the play, on a scale of 1 to 10. One set of judges
would be for the offense, and the player who gets the
higher average score for his artistry in falling down,
grunting, flailing his arms, or whatever, will be the one
who gets the free throw, while the other is charged with
the foul. In short, on a blocking-charging foul, judge
the dramatic skill, not right of way.

SOURCE: *The Essence of the Game Is Deception,* by Leonard Koppett
(Little, Brown and Company).

John Wooden's 15-Point Pyramid for Success

The record speaks for itself—10 NCAA basketball championships, including eight in nine years; 667 victories in 29 years of college coaching; an 88-game winning streak; a winning percentage of .806, third highest of all time; mentor of two of the greatest ever to play basketball, Lew Alcindor (later Kareem Abdul-Jabbar) and Bill Walton. That's what John Wooden has accomplished. Here is his success formula.

1. INDUSTRIOUSNESS. There is no substitute for work. Worthwhile things come from hard work and careful planning.
2. FRIENDSHIP. Comes from mutual esteem, respect, and devotion. A sincere liking for all.
3. LOYALTY. To yourself and to those dependent on you. Keep your self respect.
4. COOPERATION. With all levels of your co-workers. Help others and see the other side.
5. ENTHUSIASM. Your heart must be in your work. Stimulate others.
6. SELF CONTROL. Emotions under control. Delicate adjustment between mind and body. Keep judgment and common sense.
7. ALERTNESS. Be observing constantly. Be quick to spot a weakness and correct it or use it as the case may warrant.
8. INITIATIVE. Cultivate the ability to make decisions and think alone. Desire to excel.
9. INTENTNESS. Ability to resist temptation and stay

UCLA's Bill Walton, backed by Coach John Wooden, won the 1973 Sullivan Award as the best amateur athlete.   *UPI*

within your course. Concentrate on your objective and be determined to reach your goal.

10. CONDITION. Mental, moral, physical. Rest, exercise, and diet must be considered. Moderation must be practiced. Dissipation must be eliminated.

11. SKILL. A knowledge of, and the ability to, properly execute your fundamentals. Be prepared. Cover every detail.

12. TEAM SPIRIT. An eagerness to sacrifice personal interests or glory for the welfare of all. The team comes first.

13. POISE. Just being yourself. Being at ease. Never fighting yourself.

14. CONFIDENCE. Respect without fear. Confident, not cocky. May come from faith in yourself in knowing that you are prepared.

15. COMPETITIVE GREATNESS. "When the going gets tough, the tough get going." Be at your best when your best is needed. Real love of a hard battle.

SOURCE: *The Wooden-Sharman Method: A Guide To Winning Basketball* by John Wooden and Bill Sharman with Bob Seizer (MacMillan).

Walter Kennedy's All-Time NBA Team

The late Mr. Kennedy was the first public relations director of the National Basketball Association and the league's second commissioner. During his reign, the NBA rose to great heights to achieve the success it enjoys today.

Forwards—Rick Barry
           Elgin Baylor
           Joe Fulks
           Bob Pettit

Centers—Kareem Abdul-Jabbar
　　　　Wilt Chamberlain
　　　　George Mikan
　　　　Bill Russell
Guards—Bob Cousy
　　　　Walt Frazier
　　　　Oscar Robertson
　　　　Jerry West
Coach—Arnold "Red" Auerbach

SOURCE: *The Complete Handbook of Pro Basketball* (NAL Signet).

Sid Borgia's 4 Most Memorable Basketball Games

Sid Borgia, 5-8 and balding, was a strange figure among the giants of pro basketball. But, George Mikan once said, "He's just about the best official there is." Borgia refereed in the NBA from 1946 to 1966, was supervisor of NBA referees from 1961 to 1966. He refereed in more than 2,000 NBA games, missing only one game in 18 years, and officiated in eight of the league's first 14 All-Star Games.

1. The first ever NBA All-Star Game in New York's Madison Square Garden, 1946—George Mikan's West team trailed by two points in the final seconds. Slater Martin inbounded to Jim Pollard, who passed to Mikan. As he turned to shoot, Mikan was fouled by Ray Felix. Mikan went to the foul line for two shots. As he handed him the ball, Borgia said: "George, my old friend, you keep telling me I choke up. Well, you've got two free throws here and there are 18,000 people in this place who think you're the greatest thing in creation. Let's see, George, who gets the big apple on this one." P.S.: Mikan made the two fouls to tie the score, but his West team lost the game in overtime.

2. Boston Celtics vs. Syracuse Nats, War Memorial Auditorium, Feb. 19, 1959—Borgia slugged a fan who had been calling the official "gutless" and had been generally abusive all night. Borgia, in turn, was slugged by Celtic Tom Heinsohn when the ref tried to break up a fight between Heinsohn and Dolph Schayes. Bill Russell of the Celtics slugged Syracuse's George Dempsey, setting off a free-for-all between both teams, during which Heinsohn floored the Nats' Bob Hopkins and traded punches with Syracuse coach Paul Seymour. Heinsohn and teammate Gene Conley tangled with Syracuse fans before the police were summoned and broke up the melee. Says Borgia: "The fan in this situation did a job on [Celtic coach] Red Auerbach throughout the game. After the players broke up the fight between me and the fan, Red, seeing that the fan was bleeding, said to me: 'That was the only damn good thing you did all night.' Six lawyers met me at the airport after the game and told me to be prepared for a lawsuit, and the plane, a DC-3, had to make an emergency landing at LaGuardia Airport. I just couldn't win that night."

3. Game No. 7 of the Boston Celtics vs. Los Angeles Lakers playoff series, Boston Garden, April 18, 1962—With the score tied and 16 seconds left, the Celtics had the ball. Frank Ramsey took a pass and ran into Rudy LaRusso, hoping for a foul call. Borgia refused to give it to him and the Lakers had the ball with time out. Frank Selvy missed a jumper and Bill Russell grabbed the rebound as the final buzzer sounded. The Celtics won in overtime. Says Borgia: "If the Lakers had won, I'm sure even the Boston police couldn't have saved my neck from that angry crowd that night."

All-time NBA centers: Wilt Chamberlain (13) and Bill Russell (6).

Darryl Norenberg

4. Playoff Game, date unknown, between New York Knicks and Minneapolis Lakers, in Minneapolis—Borgia and Stan Stutz blew their whistles simultaneously as a shot by a Knicks player went in the air. The officials stared at one another, waiting for the other's call to avoid conflicting calls. Neither official saw the ball go in the basket and the shot was disallowed. Says Borgia: "13,000 people, including Pat Kennedy, Supervisor of Officials, and Maurice Podoloff, NBA Commissioner, saw the ball go in the basket, but not the referees. The Knicks protested the game. A hearing was held. Mr. Podoloff said, 'I don't care if Jesus Christ saw the ball go in the basket. If the refs did not see it go in, it didn't go in. Case closed.' "

Howard Garfinkel's Top 10 Pre-1951 and Top 10 Post-1951 College Basketball Teams

For the past 14 years, Howard Garfinkel, who says "It all began for me in the end balcony of the old Madison Square Garden in 1940," has been co-director of the Five-Star Basketball Camp in Honesdale, Pa., and Pittsburgh, Pa. He is a member of the selection committee for the McDonald's high school All-America team.

PRE-1951

1. Kentucky, 1947–48, Coach: Adolph Rupp—Incredible speed, depth, shooting ability, and discipline enabled Rupp's "Fabulous Five" to dominate college basketball throughout this era. I could have selected any one of the three Alex Groza-Ralph Beard-Wah Wah Jones quintets for the top spot, but indiscretions against Utah and Loyola of Chicago in the 1947 and 1948 NITs made this team the obvious choice. Support per-

formances of Cliff Barker, Kenny Rollins, Jim Line, and Dale Barnstable were indispensable for these 36–3 National champs, who also copped their fifth straight SEC title. Upon graduation, they entered the newly formed NBA as a unit (the Indianapolis Jets) and were respectable.

2. Oklahoma A&M, 1945–46, Coach: Hank Iba—Although the previous year's Aggie team beat the mighty DePaul and George Mikan in a controversial, foul-marred Red Cross benefit and nipped dangerous NYU (Tannenbaum, Forman, Schayes) in the NCAA final, this team gets the nod on superior depth because of returning war veterans. Iba's ball control style was the perfect vehicle to ride 7-0 Bob "Foothills" Kurland, Sam Aubray & Co., to back-to-back NCAA crowns, an astounding 31–2 record (58–6 over two years) and another Missouri Valley title.

3. Kentucky, 1950–51, Coach: Adolph Rupp—A new crew but the same old story for the Baron, another national championship by virtue of No. 1 rankings in both AP and UP polls and an NCAA title in a tournament field expanded to 16 teams. The 32–2 Wildcats scored a 68–58 victory over Big Seven champ Kansas State, which had conquered No. 2 Oklahoma A&M by 24 points in the Western Regional final. The Wildcats were led by 7-0 Bill Spivey, an All-America center, Frank Ramsey, later a superstar with the Boston Celtics, soph Cliff Hagan, and the depth that made the difference, Shelby Linville, Skip Whitaker, Bob Watson, and Lou Tsiropoulos.

4. St. Louis, 1947–48, Coach: Ed Hickey—The Billikens of first-year coach Hickey snapped NYU's 19-game winning streak in the NIT finals. Easy Ed Macauley, one of the great pivotmen of all time, was the fast break triggerman who outran opposition pivots. Other

key men to this 24-3 juggernaut were D.C. Wilcutt, Bob Schmidt, Dan Miller, Lou Lehman, and Marv Schatzmann. Current Marquette coach, Hank Raymonds, broke an ankle in pre-season, but returned for spot duty in the NIT.

5. CCNY, 1949-50, Coach: Nat Holman—The real City College stood up at tournament time, making their 17-5 seasonal record a sham. En route to the only Grand Slam in college history (victories in both the NCAA and NIT tournaments), CCNY defeated the nation's 12th, 6th, 5th, 3rd, 2nd and 1st ranked teams. No. 1 Bradley was the victim in the final of both events to a team comprised of Irwin Dambrot, Ed Roman, Ed Warner, Floyd Lane, and Al "Fats" Roth.

6. Wyoming, 1942-43, Coach: Ev Shelton—The Cowboys lassoed a great Georgetown team to win the NCAA crown in New York, then put that tournament on the map by beating St. John's in the first of several historic Red Cross benefit games in the Garden. Kenny Sailors, MVP of the NCAA and the finest speed dribbler and jump shooter of his day, Milo Komenich, and Don Weir were the names to remember on this underrated 31-2 powerhouse.

7. Holy Cross, 1946-47, Coach: Doggie Julian—Using Boston Garden as home base and practicing in an on-campus band box, the Crusaders marched to 23 consecutive victories (27 of 30 overall) and swept to the NCAA championship over Big 6 kingpin Oklahoma. Sparked by MVP George Kaftan, Frank Oftring, Dermot O'Connell, and a youngster named Bob Cousy, the Cross thrilled SRO Garden throngs with some of the most brilliant teamwork ever seen in the old building.

Nat Holman and the CCNY Grand Slam in 1950.

8. DePaul, 1944-45, Coach: Ray Meyer—Generally considered a one-man gang, but what a man! The legendary George Mikan, voted the greatest player of the first half of the century by an AP poll, carried teammates Stump, DiBenedetto, and Kachan on his back to the NIT championship and an impressive 21-3 record (62-12 from 1944 through 1946). Mikan smashed all tournament scoring and rebounding marks, outscoring giant Don Otten, 34-7, as DePaul beat Bowling Green in the finals.

9. LIU, 1938-39, Coach: Clair Bee—Regarded as the best coached team of its era, the unbeaten Blackbirds (a 26-game winning streak which stretched to 34 the following year) clawed undefeated Loyola of Chicago by 12 to win the NIT. To negate the then legal goaltending of center Mike Novak, the canny Bee devised an off-the-backboard shooting technique which was followed to perfection by LIU stars Dan Kaplowitz, Ossie Schectman, and Irv Torgoff. Bee's seemingly impenetrable 1-3-1 zone was another factor in the selection of this historic five.

10. Tie: St. John's, 1942-43, Coach: Joe Lapchick; Illinois, 1942-43, Coach: Doug Mills—Despite the war and freshman eligibility of High Harry Boykoff, the finest shooting big man of his day, Fuzzy Levane and Larry Baxter formed a cohesive, exciting St. John's team that typified "the City Game." Along with forwards Frank Plantamura and Al Moschetti and diminutive passing master Hy Gotkin, this team rolled to a 23-2 record and the NIT title. Boykoff, who was never the same after an Army stint, was MVP. Levane, later coach of the Knicks and St. Louis Hawks, earned the Haggerty Award as the outstanding player in New York City.

The famed Illinois "Whiz Kids" were more than a sportswriter's invention. They were undefeated (12-0) in the Big 10 and 17-1 for the year. Rated No. 1 in the land, they passed up the tournaments, making a true comparison with Wyoming and St. John's teams of that year impossible. Star guard Andy Phillip, however, could play with anyone and became a star in the NBA for 10 seasons.

POST-1951

1. UCLA, 1967-68, Coach: John Wooden—Best of 10 Wooden eligibles. Lew Alcindor (Kareem Abdul-Jabbar), Lucius Allen, Mike Warren, Lynn Shackleford, and Mike Lynn avenged their only defeat when they buried Houston and Elvin Hayes, 101-69, in the NCAA semis. Alcindor's three-year-record: 88-2.
2. San Francisco, 1954-55, Coach: Phil Woolpert—Led by the greatest team player and defender of all time, Bill Russell, the Dons extended their unbeaten streak to 55, successfully defending their NCAA crown without the heart of their backcourt, K.C. Jones, ruled ineligible for post-season play.
3. Indiana, 1975-76, Coach: Bob Knight—Knight's marauders easily defeated four teams in the top 10 (including UCLA twice and Michigan three times) en route to their 32-0 national championship. Starters Quinn Buckner, Kent Benson, Scott May, Tom Abernethy, and Bobby Wilkerson graduated to successful pro careers. Knight might have won it all two years in a row had May not been injured for the NCAA tournament.
4. UCLA, 1971-72, Coach: John Wooden—The Walton Gang was perhaps the deepest team since Rupp's "Fabulous Five," with Wilkes, Farmer, Lee, Curtis,

Hollyfield, Nater, Bibby, and Walton. The national champs licked teams by an average of 32 points per game, breaking the all-time record.

5. North Carolina State, 1973-74, Coach: Norm Sloan—If for no other reason, this team will be remembered for stopping UCLA's never-to-be-equaled string of 38 consecutive NCAA tournament victories. And they did it the hard way, coming from seven points behind in the second half. Super David Thompson, tall Tom Burleson, gritty Monte Tow, steady Moe Rivers, and tough Tom Stoddard formed the finest ACC squad in history.

6. Ohio State, 1959-60, Coach: Fred Taylor—The nation's offensive leader (90 points per game) buried defensive champ, California (50 ppg), 75-55, in the NCAA title game. The third-ranked Buckeyes of Jerry Lucas, John Havlicek, Larry Siegfried, Joe Roberts, and Mel Nowell were to gain the top spot in the polls for the next two seasons, but were upset in the NCAA finals both years.

7. North Carolina, 1956-57, Coach: Frank McGuire —Five New York City kids waylaid Wilt Chamberlain and his Kansas Jayhawks on the way to the NCAA championship in a memorable triple overtime game in Kansas City, 54-53. The Tar Heels of Lenny Rosenbluth, Joe Quigg, Tommy Kearns, Bob Cunningham, and Pete Brennan had to beat Michigan State in three overtimes in the semi-final en route to their 32-0 season.

8. UCLA, 1963-64, Coach: John Wooden—Though small by today's standards, this was the favorite five of the "Wizard of Westwood." Averaging 6-3 in height, they out-rebounded all 30 of their opponents and won the national title by beating Vic Bubas' greatest Duke team. Gail Goodrich, Walt Hazzard, and Kenny

Washington gave Wooden his first national title.

9. Duquesne, 1954–55, Coach: Dudley Moore—Led by All-Americas Sihugo Green and Dick Ricketts, Moore's "Iron Five" romped through a still-strong NIT field, which included St. Francis of Loretto and the legendary Maurice Stokes (MVP for a fourth-place team). Just as important, however, was a 67–65 triumph in the Holiday Festival final over NCAA runner-up LaSalle with Tom Gola.

10. Tie: Texas Western, 1965–66, Coach: Don Haskins; Kentucky, 1977–78, Coach: Joe B. Hall—The Miners shocked the basketball world by completing a 28–1 season with an upset of No. 1 Kentucky (Dampier-Riley) in the NCAA title game. Haskins' well-disciplined men —Bobby Joe Hill, Willie Cager, Willie Worsley, Dave Lattin, Orsten Artis, Neville Shed—who lost only to Seattle in the final regular season game at Seattle, were the first all-black team to win a major post-season championship.

Combining awesome physical power with pinpoint shooting, the modern edition of the Wildcats responded to severe media pressure to win it all in St. Louis, finishing with a 30–2 season log. Pro draft choices Goose Givens, Rick Robey, Mike Phillips, and James Lee teamed with shrewd soph floor leader Kyle Macy to out-finesse one of the strongest NCAA fields ever.

Bob Lapidus' All-Star High School Basketball Team

FIRST TEAM

F—Jerry Lucas, Middletown H.S., Middletown, Ohio, 1958

F—Connie Hawkins, Boys High, Brooklyn, N.Y., 1960

C—Lew Alcindor (Kareem Abdul-Jabbar), Power Memorial, New York, N.Y., 1964

G—Oscar Robertson, Crispus Attucks, Indianapolis, Ind., 1956

G—Calvin Murphy, Norwalk H.S., Norwalk, Conn., 1966

SECOND TEAM

F—Moses Malone, Petersburg H.S., Petersburg, Va., 1974

F—Campy Russell, Central H.S., Pontiac, Mich., 1971

C—Wilt Chamberlain, Overbrook H.S., Philadelphia, Pa., 1955

G—Jerry West, East Bank H.S., East Bank, W.Va., 1956

G—Adrian Dantley, DeMatha H.S., Hyattsville, Md., 1973

EDITOR'S NOTE: Bob Lapidus, chairman of *Scholastic* magazine's All-America Selections Board, has been following schoolboy basketball for more than 40 years. His choices start with the mid-50s, shortly before the birth of *Scholastic*'s All-America squads.

Lew Alcindor at New York's Power Memorial in 1964.
New York World-Telegram & Sun

Frank Sinatra, on assignment from *Life* magazine, shot the first Muhammad Ali-Joe Frazier fight at Madison Square Garden. *Ken Regan*

VII

The Body Beautiful

Frank Sinatra's 11 Greatest Fighters

1. Joe Louis
2. Rocky Marciano
3. Willie Pep
4. Tony Zale
5. Sugar Ray Robinson
6. Jimmy McLarnin
7. Billy Conn
8. Tony Canzoneri
9. Barney Ross
10. Muhammad Ali
11. And me!

Mr. Sinatra is a lifelong boxing fan. His father fought professionally in New Jersey under the name Marty O'Brien. His list is in no order of preference, but represents some of the many great fighters he has seen over the years.

Muhammad Ali's 10 Greatest Heavyweights

For years he kept telling us, "I am the greatest fighter of all times," but Muhammad Ali must have been bitten by the modesty bug. Shortly before becoming the first man to regain the heavyweight championship for the third time in a 15-round decision over Leon Spinks in New Orleans, Ali agreed to list the greatest heavyweights of all time. He is an inveterate film-watcher and has frequently seen the men he rates on film. His selections, which follow, are in order of preference.

1. Jack Johnson
2. Joe Louis
3. Muhammad Ali
4. Jack Dempsey
5. Rocky Marciano
6. Gene Tunney
7. Sam Langford
8. Joe Walcott
9. Floyd Patterson
10. Ezzard Charles

Don Dunphy's 12 Greatest Fights

Far and away the best boxing broadcaster in the business, Don Dunphy has broadcast the blow-by-blows of literally thousands of fights. He began his career with the first Joe Louis-Billy Conn fight in 1941, and has broadcast all the big ones since then, from Louis to Muhammad Ali. Following are his choices for greatest fights he has broadcast.

Muhammad Ali's first choice: Jack Johnson, winner of the heavyweight championship in 1908.   *UPI*

1. Rocky Graziano vs. Tony Zale (first fight)
September 27, 1946

"It's hard to pick one fight that's the greatest, but if you force me, I'll pick the first fight between Tony Zale and Rocky Graziano. This fight between an onrushing youngster and a veteran had everything, including the veteran (Zale) almost knocked out, coming from behind to score an unbelievable win."

2. Rocky Marciano vs. Jersey Joe Walcott (first fight)
September 23, 1952

"Marciano had to come from behind to win this one. Walcott, fighting a tremendous fight, had Rocky ready for the cleaners in the 12th round. In the 13th, Rocky caught Jersey Joe with the greatest single punch I've ever seen—a short right-hand smash to the jaw and Joe was out for five minutes."

3. Joe Louis vs. Billy Conn (first fight)
June 18, 1941

This was Don Dunphy's first heavyweight title fight as a broadcaster, but also an outstanding battle in which Conn was leading on points when Louis caught up with him and KOd him in the 13th round.

4. Willie Pep vs. Sandy Saddler (second fight)
February 11, 1949

"I consider the second Pep-Saddler fight a boxing classic by Pep. In a battle between two fine champions, Pep was staggered in each of the last five rounds, but by his great skill, he managed to win each of them and regained his featherweight title."

5. Ray Robinson vs. Carmen Basilio (first fight)
September 23, 1957

In this fight, Robinson lost his world middleweight title in a 15-round decision in New York. He was to regain the title from Basilio six months later in Chicago.

6. Muhammad Ali vs. Joe Frazier (first fight)
March 8, 1971

"The first Ali-Frazier was not necessarily the greatest fight, but I consider it the greatest sports event of all time. It had two undefeated heavyweight champions, Ali coming back from his anti-draft exile. I think it garnered more newspaper, radio, TV, magazine, and word-of-mouth publicity than anything ever in sports. No one who was in the Garden that night will ever forget that emotional epic." (EDITOR'S NOTE: Frazier won by a 15-round decision, Ali's first defeat.)

7. George Foreman vs. Joe Frazier (first fight)
January 22, 1973

This was the stunning upset in Kingston, Jamaica. Foreman, a heavy underdog, surprised Frazier, KOing him in two rounds to take the heavyweight title.

8. Muhammad Ali vs. Joe Frazier (third fight)
October 1, 1975

The so-called "Thriller in Manila." Ali stopped Frazier in the 14th round.

9. Ray Robinson vs. Tommy Bell
December 20, 1946

Sugar Ray won a 15-round decision in New York, to win the vacant world welterweight championship, which he held until he vacated the title and moved up to win the middleweight crown.

10. Marcel Cerdan vs. Tony Zale
September 21, 1948

Cerdan won the world middleweight championship with a 12th-round KO in Jersey City. He lost the title to Jake LaMotta nine months later.

11. Rocky Graziano vs. Billy Arnold
March 9, 1945

"I include the nontitle Graziano-Arnold because it was the beginning of one career and the end of another. Arnold battered Graziano from pillar to post for two rounds, but Rocky wouldn't go down. In the third, Graziano caught Arnold with an overhand right to finish him. He also went on to fame and fortune. Arnold disappeared."

12. Gus Lesnevich vs. Anton Christofordis
August 26, 1941

"I kiddingly pick Lesnevich and Christofordis, which was a forgettable fight for the American light heavyweight title (won by Lesnevich in a 15-round decision), but I'll always remember it. It was used as an audition to pick an announcer for the Friday night fights and I won it. Probably because I could pronounce the names."

Muhammad Ali's 8 Tips for Young Heavyweight Champions

Ali, who has been around, originally intended this for Leon Spinks, who took his title away in 1978, then lost it back to Muhammad later that year. It applies, however, to all future champions.

1. "Drive that big car until it don't run no more. The worst thing is to keep buying new cars. You can't get

your money back. They get old every year they make a new one."

2. "Get a good hunk of money, put up $20,000 for each child now, while you're making it, in case you die or get hurt or something, so their education will be paid for. Leave something for your wife. After that, your mother. Make her burdens a little lighter."

3. "Establish a nice home for your wife and your children. Don't invest in nothing, no real estate, no restaurants, no nightclubs. Put your money in government tax-free bonds, because when you retire, you still have to live; your children need money to go to school."

4. "Get yourself one lawyer and have him on standby. Don't keep him year 'round. Get a good lawyer and keep him; don't go from lawyer to lawyer and don't listen to lawyers who have one-shot deals, because those one-shot deals will kill you. There are no good deals. I'm talking from experience."

5. "When you put up money, direct the bank to use it for your children's education. Buy 50 acres of land outside some major city, some place for your family to retreat to."

6. "Don't carry a lot of cash with you because you'll give it all away to your friends. If your family or friends ask for money, give it to them, don't loan it to them. If you loan it to them, they end up your enemies. People hate you for helping them."

7. "Don't forget your wife in the midst of all the parties and the young girls hanging around you. Remember, she was with you when you weren't nothing."

8. "You're not like me. When you lose, it's all over. When I lose, I get invited to more countries. What did the man say? Loser and still champion."

Leon Spinks surprised Muhammad Ali and the world when he won the heavyweight title in Las Vegas in February 1978.   *UPI*

Gorilla Monsoon's 10 Greatest Wrestlers

1. Bruno Sammartino—"No one will ever accomplish what this man did."
2. Killer Kowalski
3. Red Bastien—"Pound for pound, one of the greatest."
4. Ivan Koloff
5. Ed "Strangler" Lewis
6. Frank Judson
7. Gorilla Monsoon
8. Yukon Eric
9. Ray Stevens and Pat Patterson
10. Bob Backlund—"Bob's career is very young, but I am sure he will prove to be one of the all-time greats."

Bob Hoffman's 10 Strongest Men

Known as "the father of world weight-lifting," Bob Hoffman organized the York Barbell Club in 1924. In 1971, his team won its 40th National AAU team championship. He is editor and publisher of *Strength & Health* magazine and president of the world-famous York Barbell Co. At 73, he is still physically active, training with weights and jogging as often as possible.

1. Vasily Alexeev—The monstrous Russian champion electrified the World of Weights by lifting 560 pounds at the Montreal Olympics in 1976. With no professional athletes in Russia to grab the spotlight, Alexeev is one of his country's biggest sports personalities.
2. Paul Anderson—As a young man, Paul surprised the world with his power when he pushed 400-plus pounds overhead. He was considered the World's Strongest

Bruno Sammartino has arm lock on Russia's Ivan Koloff.

Man, B.A. (Before Alexeev). He was the 1956 Olympic heavyweight champion. In high school, Paul played football and was considered by some opposing coaches to be the entire line.

3. Norbert Schemansky—A well-coordinated lifter with impeccable form, Norbert had the look of a professor . . . and he taught by example. He handled heavy weights smoothly and easily and was also a fine all-around athlete.

4. John Davis—John won his first world championship at age 17. He was the first American to win multiple titles. In all, he won a record-tying eight consecutive world titles.

5. Arthur Saxon—This old-timer still lives in the memory of "mighty men" throughout the world because he was the first to lift more than 400 pounds overhead with one hand. For years he traveled with circuses and did many strongman stunts with his two brothers. Many of their feats remain unbeaten to this day.

6. Louis Cyr—Another old-time strongman, this French Canadian delighted in lifting cumbersome and awkward objects, including horses and other animals. Of course, he also tried his hand with weights and, in his day, his strength defied imagination.

7. Bruce Wilhelm—A national weightlifting champion and record holder, Bruce's latest strength achievement has been winning CBS-TV's "Strongest Man in the World" competition two years running.

8. Milo Steinborn—Still another old-timer who ranks with the best, he was the first to rock 515 pounds across his shoulders and do knee bends with it. He also wrestled with the best of them for years. Now 86 years

Paul Anderson: 1956 Olympic gold medalist.

UPI

of age, he promotes wrestling and still manages to train with weights.

9. Steve Sanko—The heavy weights Steve handled in training countless times every Saturday made a lasting impression. Steve's greatest claim to fame, however, is the fact he was the first ever to total 1,000 pounds in the three Olympic lifts.

10. Bob Hoffman*—At the age of 40, he became interested in a one-hand lift called the "bent press." By the age of 53, he set an age-group record in this lift by hoisting 282 pounds overhead. Although known as "the father of world weightlifting," he is proudest of his lifting achievement because it remains untouched to this day.

*Bob Hoffman modestly omitted his own name from his list of strongmen. However, the editors of his magazine insist he belongs, and we agree.

VIII

Wheels

Reggie Jackson's 12 Most Desirable Automobiles for the Collector

It's not only home runs that baseball's Reggie Jackson collects. He has a passion for automobiles, which he collects as a hobby and business. He owns a Porsche-Audi dealership in California and collects cars, he says, "as a hedge against inflation."

Auto	Value
1. Rolls-Royce Corniche with rubber bumper, 1973–77*	$85,000
2. 375 GTB Ferrari Spider, 1973–74	$65,000–$80,000
3. 32 Fudor Phaeton, convertible, open touring car, 1932	$60,000–$70,000
4. Rolls-Royce Corniche, hardtop coupe, 1972–75*	$55,000–$70,000
5. Mercedes-Benz 6.9 four-door sedan, 1976–78*	$45,000
6. Excalibur	$33,000–$36,000

*Automobiles in Reggie Jackson's collection.

7. Turbo-Carrera Porsche, 1976–78* $35,000
8. Rolls-Royce Silver Cloud, 1964 $28,000–$35,000
9. Mercedes-Benz 280 SE Convertible, 1971 $25,000
10. Mercedes-Benz 280 SL, 1971 $15,000
11. Porsche Speedster 356, 1961 $10,000–$12,000
12. Chevrolet Bel Air, two-door, 1955* $3,000–$5,000

Al Bloemker's 10 Most Exciting Race Drivers

Al Bloemker, author of *500 Miles to Go,* is vice-president of the Indianapolis Motor Speedway. His alphabetical list covers the "most exciting drivers in open-wheel and open-cockpit championship cars on race tracks in the United States." He adds, "I've seen them all in this category for the last 55 years, and these are the 10 best 'gate attractions' of that period."

1. Mario Andretti—Tenacious
2. Ralph DePalma—Superb showman
3. Peter DePaolo—Wall-smacker and champion
4. Leon Duray—Daring and colorful
5. A.J. Foyt Jr.—King of the hill
6. Parnelli Jones—Rough and rugged
7. Rex Mays—"Charge!"
8. Tommy Milton—Supreme strategist
9. Barney Oldfield—Best of the barnstormers
10. Wilbur Shaw—"I can do anything better than you can"

(Opposite, above) Mario Andretti seems to have won everything.   *UPI*

(Opposite, below) Barney Oldfield set a world speed record of 90 miles an hour in Henry Ford's "799" in 1902. Gentleman on the right is Henry Ford.   *UPI*

MARIO ANDRETTI · 1966 · INDIANAPOLIS MOTOR SPEEDWAY

Bob Cutter's 72 Derring-Do
Auto Racers

Bob Cutter, who writes a syndicated column called "The Steering Column," has been covering automobiles and auto racing for 25 years. He is co-author of *The Encyclopedia of Auto Racing Greats* and wrote *The Complete Book of Motorcycling* and *The Model Car Handbook*.

17 MOST DARING INDIANAPOLIS DRIVERS

1. Tony Bettenhausen
2. Jimmy Bryan
3. Ralph DePalma
4. A.J. Foyt
5. Ted Horn
6. Jim Hurtubise
7. Gordon Johncock
8. Parnelli Jones
9. Rex Mays
10. Johnnie Parsons
11. Dario Resta
12. Troy Ruttman
13. Eddie Sachs
14. Wilbur Shaw
15. Bill Vukovich
16. Lee Wallard
17. Rodger Ward

Bob Cutter notes: "Daring isn't measured officially. There are no statistics, no calibrations to rely upon. It's all a matter of opinion. And there are questions: Where does daring end and foolhardiness begin? Seven of the men on this list were killed in race cars. Three are still racing. The others

A.J. Foyt has just won the 1967 Indy 500.
UPI

retired to live out their lives, or die in other ways. In compiling this list, Indy was important, but the driver's general attitude toward racing in USAC Championship cars—Indy cars to the uninitiated—was equally important. Bettenhausen, Parsons, and Vukovich, by the way, are not to be confused with Indy drivers of those names today. All these are the fathers of the drivers of today."

10 ALL-TIME WOMEN DRIVERS

1. Pat Moss Carlsson—Sister of Stirling Moss, wife of rally ace Erik Carlsson, daughter of Indy racer Alfred Moss. Perennial European Ladies Champion in Rallying, competing in more than 200 major events there and around the world. English.

2. Maria-Teresa de Filippis—The first woman to enter and compete in modern Grand Prix racing in 1958 . . . three races in all with a 10th her best finish . . . in a Maserati. The death of her mentor, Jean Behra, ended her quest. Italian.

3. Camille du Gast—The first major woman driver in the world, competing in the 1901 Paris-Berlin Race in a Panhard. She was a creditable 33rd. She switched to motorboat racing when race organizers refused the Benz team's entry of her in 1904. Died 1942. French.

4. Gwenda Glubb Hawkes—Daughter of a famed British general and sister of another, a World War I ambulance driver turned endurance driver and record-setter. English.

5. Janet Guthrie—Expert sports car driver in endurance races, became the first woman to enter the Indy 500 (1977), first to start and finish (1978). Also became a familiar figure on the NASCAR Grand National tour,

Barrier-breaking Janet Guthrie finished ninth in the 1978 Indy 500.   *UPI*

where she did well with less-than-first-class machinery. American.

6. Elizabetta Junek—A sports car ace in the 1920s at such famed contests as the Targa Florio, Swiss, and German Grands Prix (for sports cars), and others. Retired after the death of her husband-driver, 1928. Austrian.

7. Denise McCluggage—Sports car driver and rallyist, principally in the U.S. in the 1950s, with a tour of Europe. A journalist, editor of a weekly newspaper, founder of *Competition Press/Autoweek*. Retired. American.

8. Kay Petre—A Brooklands regular in the 1930s and a sports car and rally driver all over Europe. Retired. Canadian.

9. Shirley Muldowney—Probably the greatest woman drag racing star ever. First woman to gain national titles. A star attraction at the gate and in the press, rivaling Janet Guthrie, though not competing in any way in actual racing like the latter. American.

10. Elsie Wisdom—Rallyist and long-distance racer from the 1930s to the 1950s. Nicknamed "Bill" early in her career in deference to the fact that women weren't supposed to be that good. Retired. English.

15 GREATEST GRAND PRIX DRIVERS SINCE 1930

(The modern era of Formula One open-wheeled, single-seater racing started in 1930 and was formalized to its highest degree after 1950.)

1. Alberto Ascari—Son of a GP driver, the first man to win back-to-back World Driving Championships (1952–53). Killed testing a sports car, 1955. Italian.

2. Jack Brabham—Three-time champion (1959-60-66) and the only one to win in a car carrying his name. His son is now racing. Retired. Australian.

3. Rudi Caracciola—Three-time champion of Europe (equal to present World Driving Champion) with more than 225 victories over 30 years (1922–52) in all kinds of cars. Died of cancer, 1959. German.

4. Jim Clark—Two-time World Champion, winner of 25 Grands Prix, greatest GP polesitter ever (33), winner of Indianapolis 500 in 1965. Killed in Formula Two race, 1968. Scottish.

5. Nino Farina—First man crowned World Champion (1950), though he started racing 20 years before and continued until 1955. Killed in ordinary road accident, 1966. Italian.

6. Juan Fangio—Perhaps the greatest racing driver of all time. Five-time World Champion (1951–54–55–56–57) —in four different cars! Sat on GP poles 28 times, won 24 races. Retired. Argentinian.

7. Emerson Fitipaldi—Two-time World Champion (1972–74), his first being the one won by youngest driver ever. He was 25. Has won 14 Grands Prix, though not in competitive cars the last three seasons. Brazilian.

8. Graham Hill—Two-time World Champion (1962–68) and Indianapolis 500 winner in 1966. Perhaps the most gracious man in a GP cockpit. Won 14 Grands Prix. Killed in airplane crash, 1975. English.

9. Hermann Lang—Champion of Europe, 1939, his career spanned 1934–54, though the war came when he was at the peak of his career. Also a great sports car driver. Retired. German.

10. Niki Lauda—Two-time World Champion (1975–77) with 17 victories (fourth on the all-time list) in his career through 1978, all the more remarkable because he was pronounced dead in a fiery crash in 1977, but came back a contender. Italian.

11. Stirling Moss—Never won a World Championship,

but only because Fangio was his arch rival. Won 16
Grands Prix. If Fangio edged him in a GP car, he
edged Juan in a sports car. Won 194 races in his
career. Retired. English.

12. Tazio Nuvolari—Some say he was the greatest ever,
with a career spanning from 1921 to 1950. Won 70
major races. Died of TB, 1953. Italian.

13. Jackie Stewart—Three-time World Champion (1969-
71-73) with all-time GP victory total of 27 races, runner-up twice. Retired. Scottish.

14. John Surtees—Won seven motorcycle World Championships, then won 1964 World Driving Championship. Became car constructor and runs own GP team,
though retired as a driver. English.

15. Achille Varzi—Perennial champion of Italy whose career spanned from 1927 to 1948 in both sports cars
and GP racing. Killed in practice session, 1948.
Italian.

Bob Cutter adds: "A 16th man has presented his creden-
tials in 1978 and seems ready to displace someone, such as
Lang, Varzi, or Surtees.

"Mario Andretti—World Champion, 1978, with 12 career GP victories. An Indy winner, a USAC star, a sports
car ace, and now a World Champion. To join the list, he
must repeat, though there are some who say he should have
been champion in 1977 since he won the most races. Andretti expects to race in GP for another five years. He
should make the list easily."

15 ALL-TIME NASCAR STOCK CAR STARS

1. Bobby Allison—Alabama. Brother Donnie also races.
Among top 10 all-time winners with 40 victories or
more. Voted three times most popular GN driver by
fans.

2. Buck Baker—North Carolina. Son Buddy also races.

Two-time champion (1956–57). Retired and came back several times. A living legend.

3. Tim Flock—Alabama. Brother Fonty also raced. GN champion 1952, 1955. Forty career victories. Retired.

4. Bobby Isaac—North Carolina. NASCAR champion 1970. Specialist at setting records as well as racing, including closed-course stock-car record at more than 201 mph.

5. Ned Jarrett—North Carolina. Two-time champion (1961–65). Started at 17, retired early (1966) too.

6. Fred Lorenzen—Illinois. Red-haired Fearless Freddie never won a title, but often won everything else not nailed down. Retired, but returned to win some more, 37 victories in all. Now retired for good.

7. Junior Johnson—North Carolina. Never a champion, but won 50 Grand Nationals all the same. So colorful, they made a movie about his life, from moonshining to race car managing. Retired.

8. David Pearson—South Carolina. The Silver Fox won three NASCAR titles (1966–68–69) and 97 races through 1978. Second on all lists only to Richard Petty.

9. Lee Petty—North Carolina. Another three-time winner (1954–58–59), father of Richard. Lee won 54 GN races, third to his son and David Pearson. Retired.

10. Richard Petty—North Carolina. Lee's son has won the most races of anyone in NASCAR history and he could reach 200 with a couple of hot years. He holds about every record there is in major stock-car racing.

11. Fireball Roberts—Florida. The nickname came from his prowess as a fastball pitcher as a youth, but Glenn Roberts was also a fast driver. He won 32 races, set records everywhere, even finished in the top 10 at the famed LeMans 24-hour race. Killed at Darlington, 1964.

12. Herb Thomas—North Carolina. Champion 1951–53, runner-up three other seasons. Won 49 GN races in his career. One of the original NASCAR drivers. Retired.

13. Curtis Turner—Virginia. The records say he won 17, but there were other seasons like 1956, when Turner won 22 convertible NASCAR races. All told, he won 360 races in and out of NASCAR ranks. Killed in airplane crash, 1970.

14. Joe Weatherly—Virginia. Two-time champion (1962–63) with 24 career victories. Killed at Riverside Raceway, 1964.

15. Cale Yarborough—South Carolina. Only man in NASCAR history to win three consecutive GN titles (1976–77–78). He is now at the peak of his career, and he could threaten every record and driver except Richard Petty as all-time winner.

15 MOST VERSATILE MODERN DRIVERS

1. Mario Andretti—What needs to be said more than this: World Driving Champion, 1978; winner of the Indianapolis 500; winner of the Daytona 500, grand-daddy of NASCAR races; winner of the Sebring 12 hours, traditional sports car battle; winner in midgets, sprints, Formula 5000, at anything he has cared to try. Italian-born, naturalized American.

2. Mark Donohue—He started in sports cars and excelled; he raced TransAm sedans and won championships; he raced USAC and won many, including the 1972 Indy 500; he raced stock cars and won; he raced one of the fastest, trickiest cars ever conceived—the Porsche 917-10—and won championships; and he raced Grand Prix cars. Killed in European race, 1975. American.

3. George Follmer—Another sports car star who moved on to bigger and better things. He started in, of all

things, gymkhanas, moved on to sports, stock, and endurance races. He won TransAm and CanAm championships. He raced Formula One. American.

4. A.J. Foyt—Versatile as he chose, he starred in midget, sprint, stock, and USAC cars. The only man to win four Indy 500-milers. Perennial USAC National Champion. And he dabbled in some other things, winning, along the way, the famed LeMans 24-hour race (with Dan Gurney) among others. The Man from Texas can win anything he really wants. American.

5. Dan Gurney—The All-America boy from Long Island and California. Sports cars, Grand Prix cars (including his own design Eagles), USAC, endurance races such as LeMans (where he co-drove a Ford to victory with Foyt), CanAm, stock cars. Retired. American.

6. Graham Hill—He started racing late, but his was a great talent. Principally a Grand Prix ace (and two-time World Champion), he also could drive anything and win when he did. Indy in 1966. Endurance races such as the Tourist Trophy. Bonneville Salt Flats to amass a series of closed-course records. Killed in a private airplane crash, 1975. English.

7. Phil Hill—The first American World Driving Champion (1961), who was one of the best endurance drivers ever, including repeat victories at LeMans, Daytona, Sebring, Nurburgring, and others. Retired as an active driver, he can still win historic car races. American.

8. David Hobbs—The TV commentator who happens to be fast in whatever you give him—from sports cars, to GT racing cars in IMSA's big series, to USAC Championship cars, to stock cars, to CanAm, to Formula 5000, in which he won the U.S. championship. English.

9. Bruce McLaren—He was a Grand Prix driver of no mean talent, and even had his own team of cars built

to his design. But the man's greatest feats came in the Canadian-American Challenge Cup, where he won as driver and designer repeatedly, and in the Australia-New Zealand Tasman Series, in which he thrilled the home folks. Killed testing a new car, 1970. New Zealander.

10. Stirling Moss—A Grand Prix star who never won the World Championship because his contemporary was five-time winner Juan Fangio, he outstarred Fangio in sports cars in epic duels. He also raced everything from 500cc cars to the biggest, brashest sports cars and prototypes equally well, winning 194 of 466 major starts. His 1955 Mille Miglia victory is remembered as one of motor racing's greatest feats (the length of the Italian peninsula at an average speed of 100 mph without stop except for fuel). Retired. English.

11. Danny Ongais—A drag racing star, who also dabbled in motorcycles, he took up car racing late. Sports cars first, then USAC Championship cars, starring in 1978 with the greatest number of victories on the Championship Trail, even as he also starred in CanAm racing. Hawaiian-American.

12. Sam Posey—A brash, talkative, and talented endurance driver, who also could handle open-wheelers well, including Formula One and Formula 5000. He also starred in sports racers in IMSA, was known to cut hot laps at Bonneville, and in TransAm, CanAm, and other forms of the sport. American.

13. Brian Redman—A sports and endurance driver who also tried Formula One, CanAm, and other forms of European sport with equal success—winning at Sebring, Spa, Nurburgring, Watkins Glen, and points East and West. Then came a second career as a CanAm star. English.

14. Johnny Rutherford—Texas like Foyt, and almost as

versatile. USAC's many categories, stock cars, sports cars, endurance races . . . and Indy 500 victories, 1974 and 1976. American.

15. Peter Revson—Sports cars, then Formula Junior (pint-sized GP cars), then through the European open-wheeler categories—Formula Three, Two, and, finally, Formula One, winning all the while. Sports racers and CanAm championships, USAC victories. Killed in a race, 1974. American.

IX

Making Love,
in the Rough

Bill Tilden's 6 Sexist Tips for
Mixed Doubles Play

Big Bill Tilden was named in a poll by the Associated Press as the greatest tennis player of the half-century.

1. Hit at the girl whenever possible.
2. A sudden shift down the man's sideline, particularly if made by the girl, will often pay.
3. One player up and one back, which is fatal in men's doubles, is a safe and, at times, sound formation in mixed. Take your pick of who's up and who's back.
4. The lob over the girl's head is one of the best shots in mixed doubles, provided you play it far enough to her side so that she has to cover it or make the man run a long way to save her.
5. The middle shot in mixed is not so good, since the man is usually covering center court.
6. Speed to the girl, finesse to the man, will pay in the

Bill Tilden: A giant in the Golden Twenties. *UPI*

mixed game. Remember that a girl's fastest shot is a man's average pace, so if you use real speed against her, it will prove a tremendous pressure under which she is apt to break. The man is tuned to speed, so fool him by finesse.

SOURCE: *How To Play Better Tennis*, by William T. Tilden (Simon & Schuster).

Bobby Riggs' 6 Handicaps for Court Hustlers

Winner of the Nationals in 1939, Bobby Riggs has spent the last quarter of a century playing tennis for fun and profit.

1. Carrying an open umbrella in my left hand, even when serving.
2. Carrying a weighted suitcase in my left hand, also when serving.
3. Wearing an oversized overcoat, buttoned from neck to ankle, and heavy rubber galoshes.
4. Burdened by weights around my waist, wrist, and ankles.
5. Tied with rope to my doubles partner, chain-gang style, to cut down our court coverage.
6. Holding a leash with a dog—or two dogs—at the other end.

SOURCE: *Court Hustler*, by Bobby Riggs with George McGann (Lippincott).

No handicap was too great for hustling Bobby Riggs.   *UPI*

Bud Collins' 25 Greatest Men and Women Tennis Players, 1941–1978

As television commentator, newspaper columnist, and author, Bud Collins has played a significant role in the tennis explosion. His selections will appear in the forthcoming *Bud Collins Tennis Encyclopedia*.

(Listed Alphabetically)

1. Pauline Betz
2. Bjorn Borg
3. Louise Brough
4. Maria Bueno
5. Maureen Connolly
6. Jimmy Connors
7. Margaret Smith Court
8. Margaret Osborne du Pont
9. Roy Emerson
10. Chris Evert
11. Althea Gibson
12. Pancho Gonzalez
13. Doris Hart
14. Lew Hoad
15. Billie Jean King
16. Jack Kramer
17. Rod Laver
18. Ilie Nastase
19. John Newcombe
20. Ken Rosewall
21. Manuel Santana
22. Frank Sedgman
23. Pancho Segura
24. Vic Seixas
25. Tony Trabert

Allison Danzig's 15 Greatest Men and 10 Greatest Women Tennis Players, 1914–1941

Mr. Danzig was, for many years, tennis expert of the *New York Times*.

(Listed in Order of Preference)

MEN

1. Bill Tilden
2. Henri Cochet
3. Don Budge
4. Jean Rene Lacoste
5. Fred Perry
6. Ellsworth Vines
7. Billy Johnston
8. Norman Brookes
9. Jean Borotra
10. Jack Crawford
11. Baron Gottfried von Cramm
12. Maurice McLaughlin
13. Bobby Riggs
14. Tony Wilding
15. Richard Norris Williams

WOMEN

1. Suzanne Lenglen
2. Helen Wills Moody
3. Alice Marble
4. Helen Jacobs
5. Dorothea Lambert Chambers
6. Molla Mallory
7. Kitty McKane Godfree
8. Sarah Palfrey Danzig
9. Dorothy Round
10. Betty Nuthall

Southpaw Rod Laver won the Wimbledon crown four consecutive times.
UPI

Al Laney's 16 Greatest Men and 10 Greatest Women Tennis Players, 1914–1941

Mr. Laney was a longtime tennis writer for the *New York Herald Tribune* and the *Paris Herald* and is one of the game's foremost experts.

(Listed Alphabetically)

MEN

1. Jean Borotra
2. Norman Brookes
3. Jacques Brugnon
4. Don Budge
5. Henri Cochet
6. Baron Gottfried von Cramm
7. Jack Crawford
8. Billy Johnston
9. Rene Lacoste
10. Maurice McLaughlin
11. Fred Perry
12. Bobby Riggs
13. Bill Tilden
14. Ellsworth Vines
15. Tony Wilding
16. Dick Williams

WOMEN

1. Mary K. Browne
2. Dorothea Lambert Chambers
3. Sarah Palfrey Danzig
4. Kitty McKane Godfree
5. Helen Jacobs

Suzanne Lenglen brought Gallic fire and the grace of a ballet dancer to the game she ruled as a six-time Wimbledon champion.   *UPI*

6. Suzanne Lenglen
7. Molla Mallory
8. Alice Marble
9. Helen Wills Moody
10. Dorothy Round

Lance Tingay's 7 Greatest Left-Handed Tennis Players

Lance Tingay of the *London Daily Telegraph* has been covering tennis since 1932 and he has seen the world's best players, both left-handed and right-handed. He has seen every minute of every match played at Wimbledon since 1955 and is the author of two books on tennis, *100 Years of Wimbledon* and *The Pictorial History of Lawn Tennis*.

1. Rod Laver
2. Norman Brookes
3. Jimmy Connors
4. Neale Fraser
5. Jaraslov Drobny
6. Arthur Larsen
7. Ann Jones

The Top 10 Men and Top 10 Women Celebrity Tennis Players

MEN

1. Robert Duvall, actor ("The Godfather"). A disciplined stylist with strong basic strokes, he plays tennis like the tough characters he portrays in films.
2. George Plimpton, author (*Paper Lion*). A life-long player who possesses a polished all-around game. Alan

Bill Cosby plays even better with a cigar in his mouth.   *UPI*

King jokes that he has "a $1.25 backhand to show for $400,000 worth of lessons."

3. Bruce Jenner, 1976 Olympic decathlon champ, TV personality. Only took up the game after the Olympics, but his outstanding athletic ability has quickly made this left-hander an agile, hard-hitting player.

4. Ron Ely, actor ("Tarzan" TV series). Owner of a bullet serve that's probably the fastest among celebrities, he uses his 6-foot, 5-inch reach to good advantage at the net, too.

5. Oleg Cassini, designer. Once a top-ranked junior in his native Italy, his finesse and court savvy make him a desirable doubles partner. And he remains in remarkable shape for a man of 65.

6. James Caan, actor ("The Godfather," "Brian's Song"). A professional rodeo rider, he's aggressive and quick on court. "Jimmy's a cocky player," says one friend, "but it works for him."

7. Bill Cosby, comedian. A good, but not great, athlete as many believe, he's devoted to the game. Tends to be erratic and temperamental, but, when things are right, he can be formidable on court.

8. Peter Benchley, author (*Jaws, The Deep*). An ex-high school All-American swimmer who has sound, clean strokes and a canny command of strategy. Weakness: return of serve.

9. Ted Kennedy, politician. Hampered by a bad back, which restricts his maneuverability, especially when he's tired. But he is, nonetheless, a strong player who's tough under pressure.

10. William Clay Ford, businessman (Ford Motor scion, Detroit Lions owner). Nationally ranked while at Yale, he still moves around the court with agility and plays to win. Also a 2-handicap golfer.

WOMEN

1. Cathy Lee Crosby, actress ("The Coach," ex-TV "Wonder Woman"). Held a national ranking as a junior and played at Wimbledon. She has a fine all-around game with a strong backhand and volley.
2. Barbara Anderson, actress ("Ironside" TV series). A consistent player with steady strokes, she has a good court sense and a cool, aggressive attitude.
3. Sheila Young, speed skater and cyclist (winner of three medals at the 1976 Olympics). Confident and poised, she covers a lot of court and attacks well.
4. Elke Sommer, actress ("A Shot in the Dark," "The Oscar"). Years of court experience have endowed her with solid strokes and good ball sense. Plays with power and competitive fire.
5. Farrah Fawcett-Majors, actress ("Charlie's Angels") and cover girl. A steady backcourt player with an impressive serve and a reliable two-handed backhand. Lots of enthusiasm and stamina.
6. Cheryl Tiegs, model. She's a natural athlete who leaps around the court and makes good use of her 5-foot 10-inch height. "Very distracting to play against her," says one male friend.
7. Helen Reddy, singer. A native Australian with good coordination who plays a lot on the court she and her husband have installed at home. Has solid strokes and moves well.
8. Ethel Kennedy, founder of RFK Pro-Celebrity Tournament. Scrappy, she always seems to get the ball back. "Ethel could have won on the pro circuit," quips Alan King, "if she could have called her own lines."
9. Katherine Graham, publisher (the *Washington Post, Newsweek*). Makes good use of years of experience, playing a consistent game at the baseline and moving well to the net when necessary.

10. Dinah Shore, singer, TV hostess. A veteran, court-wise player who has a great knowledge of the game, dependable strokes and a knack for playing the percentages.

EDITOR'S NOTE: Only recreational players were considered for the list; actors Vincent Van Patten and Dean Martin Jr. were disqualified, for example, because they have played professionally.

SOURCE: *Tennis* magazine, a publication of the New York Times Co.

7 Golfers' Approach to an 'Umbling Game

Jack Nicklaus is said to put his pants on one leg at a time. Whether that makes him superstitious or mere mortal is a matter for debate, but here is what some other noted golfers do to ward off shanks, hooks, and the double bogey man.

1. Gary Player: "I wear black. I loved Westerns and the cowboys always looked good in black."
2. Chi Chi Rodriguez: "I don't like No. 3 balls. I always mark my balls with heads and always carry two nickels to do it. I used to wear green on Sundays because it is the color of money. Now I wear red because it is the color I like to see on the board."
3. George Archer: "I don't like No. 4 balls. And I don't like fives, sixes, or sevens on my cards."
4. Hubert Green: "I don't wear yellow. I think it's a passive color."
5. Al Geiberger: "I mark my ball with a penny. If I am having a hot streak, I'll make sure to mark my ball with the same side each time; if I'm going badly, I'll reserve it. Or I'll make sure that Lincoln's eyes are pointed toward the hole before I line up my next shot."
6. Sandra Palmer: "I like to get up three hours before I

Farrah Fawcett-Majors makes the Top 10 on every count. *UPI*

play no matter what time of day it is. And I usually avoid No. 3 balls."

7. Tom Watson: "If I shoot a good round one day, I'll eat the same thing for dinner that I had the night before. I always carry three coins in my pocket and also three tees—just three—in my right pocket. I always use a broken tee on par 3 holes."

Joe Schwendeman's 2 Greatest Left-Handed Golfers

In more than 20 years as a golf writer for the *Philadelphia Bulletin* and *Philadelphia Inquirer*, Schwendeman got to cover all the big tournaments, leading pros and the rare left-handers. He is currently director of communications for the PGA Tour.

1. Bob Charles of New Zealand is the greatest lefty because he won five events on the PGA Tour, plus the 1963 British Open, four New Zealand Opens, two Swiss Opens, the 1973 South African Open, and a half-dozen other events. He was, and is, an outstanding putter, too.

2. Sam Adams of Boone, N.C., brings up the rear of this select list. A regular on the PGA Tour, he won the 1973 Quad Cities Open.

Schwendeman adds: "Great southpaw golfers are more scarce than a clean day in Los Angeles. When lefties take up golf, they are almost always changed into right-handed golfers. Why? No one knows for sure except left-handed clubs are rare and golf teachers are right-handed and just can't seem to bring themselves to teach golfers 'who hit from the wrong side of the ball.' The most famous golfer who was and is a natural lefty is Ben Hogan. Bobby Jones also threw baseballs left-handed."

Despite the seeming wince, Gary Player is winner of 50,000 in the 1968 World Series of Golf at Akron, Ohio.
UPI

X

Winter Games

Phil Esposito's 10 Superstitions

1. ITALIAN HORNS/EVIL EYE (*mal'occhio*). "I've been under this curse for the last year-and-a-half, but my great aunt (94 years old) in Sault Ste. Marie is working on removal of the evil eye."

2. ALWAYS WEAR A TURTLENECK UNDER YOUR HOCKEY SWEATER. "I was the first player in the NHL to do this. It's my trademark."

3. ALWAYS SIT IN AISLE SEAT IN AIRPLANE, NEVER AT THE WINDOW. "Did you ever hear of a plane crashing in the middle?"

4. NEVER SIGN AUTOGRAPHS BEFORE A GAME. "It seems we always lose when I sign before a game. But sometimes it's impossible to say no."

5. NO CROSSED STICKS IN DRESSING ROOM. "I'd rather see a black cat in front of my locker."

Phil Esposito would feel naked without his turtleneck. *Robert Shaver*

6. ALWAYS DRESS RIGHT TO LEFT. "Unfortunately, I have only one head."
7. NEVER USE OLD SUPPLIES. ". . . a fresh pack of gum, fresh tape—one roll black friction; two rolls 1½ inch medical; one roll 2-inch medical."
8. POST AS MANY GOOD LUCK CHARMS AS POSSIBLE . . . ALL FAITHS AND BELIEFS IF POSSIBLE. "I have these all over my locker area: four-leaf clovers, Jewish star, Chinese good luck charm. I can't afford to offend anyone. You know, there was a Chinese hockey player once. He played for the Rangers, in fact. And there are some other Chinese players in junior hockey in Canada."
9. IF WE WIN, WEAR THE SAME SUIT THE NEXT GAME. "Not a very good idea when you play four games in five nights, but it works for me."
10. KEEP IN TOUCH WITH GREAT AUNT AT LEAST ONCE A MONTH. "Make sure she's still working on removing the *mal'occhio* from me."

Gordie Howe's All-Time Hockey Team of Teammates and Opponents

Gordie Howe, it seems, has been in professional hockey almost as long as there has been a league in which to play. For 25 years (1946–71), he played in the NHL with the Detroit Red Wings. After a two-year layoff, he returned at age 45 to play for the Houston Aeros of the WHA. At the age of 50, he and sons Mark and Marty switched to the New England Whalers. The elder Howe holds almost every career scoring record worth holding, and then some. His all-time team is chosen from among those players he has played with, or against.

Goalies—Terry Sawchuk, Detroit Red Wings, Toronto

Bobby Orr, the boy wonder from Parry Sound, Ontario, was a star from the moment they played the National Anthem (Canada and U.S.) at his first National Hockey League game.   *Dick Raphael*

Maple Leafs, Los Angeles Kings, New York Rangers

Bill Durnan, Montreal Canadiens

Defensemen—Bobby Orr, Boston Bruins, Chicago Black Hawks

Red Kelly, Detroit Red Wings, Toronto Maple Leafs

Doug Harvey, Montreal Canadiens, New York Rangers, St. Louis Blues

Bill Gadsby, Chicago Black Hawks, New York Rangers, Detroit Red Wings*

Centers—Phil Esposito, Chicago Black Hawks, Boston Bruins, New York Rangers

Jean Beliveau, Montreal Canadiens

Milt Schmidt, Boston Bruins

Stan Mikita, Chicago Black Hawks

Right Wings—Maurice "Rocket" Richard, Montreal Canadiens

Bernie "Boom Boom" Geoffrion, Montreal Canadiens, New York Rangers

Andy Bathgate, New York Rangers, Toronto Maple Leafs, Detroit Red Wings, Pittsburgh Penguins

Guy Lafleur, Montreal Canadiens*

Left Wings—Ted Lindsay, Detroit Red Wings, Chicago Black Hawks

Bobby Hull, Chicago Black Hawks, Winnipeg Jets

*Says Howe: "Gadsby and Lafleur are picked because of personal reasons. Guy is just too damned good to leave off any damned team, as is Bill, who played 20 years, enjoying all-star recognition without the joy of being a Stanley Cup winner."

EDITOR'S NOTE: Howe played with and against Gadsby, but never had the pleasure of doing either with Lafleur.

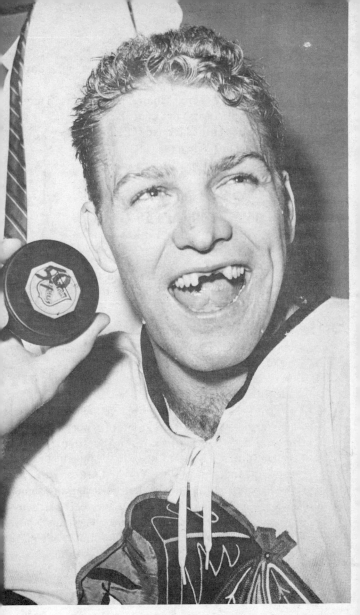

Missing teeth and the 50-goal puck were among Bobby Hull's
trademarks.   *UPI*

Johnny Bucyk, Detroit Red Wings, Boston Bruins

Dickie Moore, Montreal Canadiens, Toronto Maple Leafs, St. Louis Blues

Swingmen—Marty and Mark Howe, Houston Aeros, New England Whalers

John Halligan's 10 Greatest Hockey Flakes

John Halligan knows about hockey and flakes. He is the longtime Director of Public Relations for the New York Rangers.

1. Gilles Gratton—Reincarnated as a goalie after being a soldier in the Spanish Inquisition; hockey's first streaker and first concert pianist.
2. Derek Sanderson—There are those who could have made a living on the $100 bills he burned.
3. Tiny Tim—He loved hockey even before Miss Vickie.
4. Phil Watson—Watson to a group of reporters: "Gentlemen, I have nothing to say. Any questions?"
5. Fern Gauthier—They said he couldn't put the puck in the ocean and, from New York's Battery Park, he proved them right. His first shot hit a parking sign.
6. Howie Young—His madcap career covered 13 seasons, countless penalty boxes, and reams of newspaper copy.
7. Eddie Shore—When players on his team didn't play, they sold popcorn or changed light bulbs in the arena.
8. Jerry Mitchell—The *New York Post* reporter who described a penalty shot as "a drink with a bar pest."

9. Bob Plager—One of modern-day hockey's premier practical jokers.

10. Gary Simmons—He once bought an expensive saddle, although he didn't own a horse.

Bill Chadwick's All-Time Hockey Team

Hall of Fame referee Bill Chadwick blew his whistle for 16 years in the NHL, from 1940 through 1955. He invented the hand signals referees use today. Since 1968, he has been the color commentator for the New York Rangers.

He says in his autobiography, *The Big Whistle*, "Now I know I'm going to get some flack on my team from a lot of people, especially my friends in the press box who hear from me when they pick the wrong stars of the game. They'll be asking, 'What about the moderns—the Phil Espositos and Bobby Orrs?' Well, this is my team from my era when I was a referee. My squad numbers 11 players, and even though that's more than you'd expect to find, I'm not going to reduce it. I'm the referee in this game and we're playing by my rules."

Goalie—Bill Durnan, Montreal Canadiens, 1943–50: The finest goaltender I ever saw. He was ambidextrous and could switch the stick from side to side.

Goalie—Turk Broda, Toronto Maple Leafs, 1936–52: My playoff choice. Broda was a funny man, a happy-go-lucky sort of an individual, and I imagine that helped him as a goalie.

Defenseman—Jack Stewart, Detroit Red Wings-Chicago Black Hawks, 1938–52: A tremendous competitor. When he saw Milt Schmidt, Stewart would try to knock him down.

Defenseman—Dit Clapper, Boston Bruins, 1927-47: He'd stand up there at the blue line and challenge a forward to get by him.

Defenseman—Red Kelly, Detroit Red Wings-Toronto Maple Leafs, 1947-67: He was a tremendous puck handler.

Defenseman—Doug Harvey, Montreal Canadiens-New York Rangers-Detroit Red Wings-St. Louis Blues, 1947-69: In my opinion, there has never been a better playmaker among defensemen. Harvey was a genius on the power play.

Center—Milt Schmidt, Boston Bruins, 1936-55: My favorite, a tremendous skater and fabulous playmaker. Milt had more guts than any player in the league. He was, and is, a high-class guy.

Center—Jean Beliveau, Montreal Canadiens, 1950-71: Beliveau had finesse. He was a marvelous skater. He had class and was a shade above the other players.

Right Wing—Maurice "Rocket" Richard, Montreal Canadiens, 1942-60: Richard was in a class by himself. Rocket had a nose for the goal and from the blue line in he would explode. Rocket was a mean guy on and off the ice. He'd take somebody's eye out to score a goal.

Right Wing—Gordie Howe, Detroit Red Wings-Houston Aeros-New England Whalers, 1946-71, 1973-forever: If I wanted to win, Gordie Howe is it. A classic hockey player who can do everything well.

Left Wing—Ted Lindsay, Detroit Red Wings-Chicago

What goalies always remembered about Maurice "Rocket" Richard were his eyes. "When he came at you with a puck on his stick, his eyes were all lit up, flashing and gleaming like a pinball machine," said Glenn Hall.
Scotty Kilpatrick

Black Hawks, 1944–60, 1964–65: Lindsay was
the best left wing I saw. He was simply a mean
hockey player, a nasty individual on the ice.
But he made it pay off for him.
Coach—Hap Day, Toronto Maple Leafs, 1940–50: An in-
telligent individual and a good handler of men.

SOURCE: *The Big Whistle*, by Bill Chadwick with Hal Bock (Hawthorn).

Marv Albert's 6 Most Memorable Sudden-Death Hockey Games

Marv Albert, sports director of WNBC-TV, covers national
college basketball and pro football for the network and is
the radio voice of the New York Rangers hockey team and
the New York Knickerbockers basketball team.

1. 1977 Stanley Cup clincher for Montreal Canadiens over
   the Boston Bruins
   A goal by Jacques Lemaire gave Habs a 4–0 series sweep.

2. New York Islanders and New York Rangers, Game 3 of
   the first-round playoff, 1975
   J.P. Parise scored in 11 seconds of overtime to break a
3–3 tie following a Brad Park giveaway. The Rangers had
scored three goals in the final period of regulation time to
tie it. This was the deciding game and Parise's goal marked
the moment of ascension for the Islanders and the collapse
of Emile Francis' Rangers.

3. Detroit vs. Montreal Maroons, first-round playoff, 1936
   This was the longest game ever. It was a scoreless game
through regulation and through five overtime periods of 20
minutes each. Finally, with 3:30 left in the sixth overtime,
rookie Mud Bruneteau, who had scored only two goals all
season, beat goalie Lorne Chabot to give Detroit a 1–0 vic-

tory. Detroit goalie Hooley Smith had 90 saves. The game lasted five hours and 50 minutes and the winning goal came at 2:25 a.m.

4. New York Rangers vs. Chicago Black Hawks, in Game
     6 of the 1971 semi-finals
This was a triple overtime, the game ending near midnight. The Rangers' Pete Stemkowski put in a rebound at 1:29 of the third overtime to give his side a 3–2 victory that evened the series at three games apiece. But the Black Hawks won the deciding game at home, 4–2, to take the series.

5. New York Rangers vs. Montreal Maroons, Game 2,
     1928
Ranger goalie Lorne Chabot was cut and forced to leave the game in the third period of a 1–1 tie. The Rangers asked for permission to take a spare goalie out of the stands, but the Maroons denied the request. Half facetiously, it was suggested to Ranger coach Lester Patrick that he don the pads and take over for Chabot. With no other choice, Patrick, at age 42, accepted the challenge. He held the Maroons scoreless in the third and the game went into overtime. After seven minutes and five seconds, Frank Boucher scored to give the Rangers a 2–1 victory and they eventually went on to win the Stanley Cup.

6. New York Rangers vs. Montreal Canadiens, Game 4,
     1967
Down three games to none, the Rangers played the powerful Canadiens scoreless for the full regulation time of Game 4. In overtime, Ranger Red Berenson, a former Canadien who had not scored a goal all season, skated in on Montreal goalkeeper Rogatien Vachon, faked him out and shot at an open net. The victory might have helped the

Rangers turn things around, but Berenson's shot hit the post and gave the Canadiens a life. Eventually, it was John Ferguson, later to become coach of the Rangers, who scored the goal that gave the Canadiens the overtime victory and a sweep of the four-game series.

SOURCE: *The Complete Handbook of Pro Hockey* (NAL Signet).

All-Time Listing of the Leading Point Scorers in Hockey History Whose Names Begin With Each Letter of the Alphabet, NHL and WHA, Through the 1977–78 Season

	G.	A.	Pts.
A—George Armstrong	322	451	773
B—Johnny Bucyk	597	875	1,472
C—Yvan Cournoyer	490	493	983
D—Alex Delvecchio	491	894	1,385
E—Phil Esposito	684	841	1,525
F—Bill Flett	268	259	528
G—Rod Gilbert	440	648	1,088
H—Gordie Howe	1,033	1,466	2,499
I—Earl Ingarfield	188	234	422
J—Busher Jackson	259	246	505
K—Dave Keon	455	653	1,108
L—Ted Lindsay	426	521	947
M—Stan Mikita	579	976	1,552
N—Bob Nevin	326	439	765
O—Bobby Orr	294	709	1,003
P—Dean Prentice	404	486	890
Q—Bill Quackenbush	62	222	284
R—Henri Richard	407	768	1,175
S—Fred Stanfield	285	390	675
T—Marc Tardif	385	414	799
U—Norm Ullman	568	881	1,449

V—Carol Vadnais	153	354	507
W—Ed Westfall	247	418	665
X—			
Y—Tim Young	71	135	206
Z—Mike Zuke	28	41	69

EDITOR'S NOTE: There has never been a hockey player whose last name began with the letter "X."

SOURCE: Jim Poris and *The Complete Encyclopedia of Ice Hockey* (Prentice-Hall).

John Caldwell's 10 Greatest U.S. Cross-Country Skiers

John Caldwell, author of *The Cross-Country Ski Book* and *Caldwell on Cross-Country,* teaches mathematics and coaches skiing at the Putney School in Vermont. He was a member of the United States Olympic Ski team in 1952, a former U.S. ski coach, and is now coaches' development coordinator for the U.S. Ski Assn. His list is alphabetical.

1. Tim Caldwell
2. Larry Damon
3. Stan Dunklee
4. Mike Elliott
5. Bob Gray
6. Mike Gallagher
7. Bill Koch
8. Mack Miller
9. Martha Rockwell
10. Alison Spencer

Archer Winsten's 10 Favorite Ski Areas, Domestic and Foreign

Archer Winsten, movie critic and ski editor of the *New York Post,* was born in Seattle, Wash., in 1904, and born

to skiing in 1941. He has been skiing ever since, having skied the East, the West, Alaska, Austria, Switzerland, France, Italy, and New York City's Van Cortlandt Park "when they had rope tows there." And, he adds, "I'm still active."

1. Hunter Mountain, N.Y.—Because it's closest, makes better snow, and grooms it better.
2. Aspen, Colo.—Because Everyman can be his own expert on Snowmass.
3. Tuckerman Ravine, N.H.—The ultimate test of guts, technique, and endurance.
4. Alta, Utah—The great kept intimate, with Snowbird next door.
5. Killington, Vt.—Because it never stops growing, 3½-mile ski lift, 5-mile trail.
6. Vail, Colo.—Because it's so big, bland, popular.
7. Jackson Hole, Wyo.—Not too crowded, but with mostest for the dedicated.
8. Cortina d'Ampezzo, Italy—Because it has variety of slope, charm of people.
9. Val d'Isere, France—Because Killy started here and the terrain's terrific.
10. Plattekill, N.Y.—Because it has the family style the way it used to be at small areas.

Archer Winsten adds: "Also the Bugaboos, Monashees, Cariboos, Bobbie Burns, and Selkirks because they're the ultimate in helicopter skiing and I've never been there and probably never will. And there are 100 other places just as good as the above list simply because there's skiing."

Bill Koch won a silver medal for the U.S. in cross-country at the 1976 Winter Olympic Games.   *UPI*

Rudi Mattesich's 11 Greatest Places To Ski Tour

Seventy-six-year-old Rudi Mattesich, president and founder of the Ski Touring Council and author of several books, is responsible for the Council's *Guide* and *Schedule,* which are among the most comprehensive and informative books on touring in the East. He lives in Troy, Vt.

1. Grantham, N.H. 03753, Grey Ledges
2. Lake Placid, N.Y. 12946, Adirondack Loj
3. Wilmington, N.Y. 12997, Whiteface Chalet (near Lake Placid)
4. Inlet, N.Y. 13360, Inlet Ski Touring Center
5. East Burke, Vt. 05832, Darion Inn Ski Touring Center
6. Brookfield, Vt. 05036, Green Trails Ski Touring Center
7. Chittenden, Vt. 05737, Mountain Top Ski Touring Center
8. Craftsbury Common, Vt. 05827, Ski Touring Center, The Inn on the Common
9. Killington, Vt. 05751, Mountain Meadows Ski Touring Center
10. Northfield, Me. 01360, Northfield Mountain Ski Touring Center
11. Kingfield, Me. 04947, Deer Farm Ski Touring Center

Hans Gmoser's 6 Favorite Helicopter Ski Runs

An accomplished skier and mountain guide, Hans Gmoser pioneered helicopter skiing in the Canadian Rockies. He is president of Canadian Mountain Holidays, which makes it possible for skiers to fly by helicopter to challenging peaks not available by cable car or chairlift.

1. Bills Pass in the Bugaboos
2. Route 66 in the Bugaboos
3. Jumbo Ruji in Radium
4. Sunde in Radium
5. Purple Heart in the Bobbie Burns
6. Porpoise in the Bobbie Burns

The National Ski Patrol's 10 Most Dramatic Rescues

1. The rescue on April 15, 1978, by the Squaw Valley Ski Patrol of 37 survivors (there were four fatalities) from an aerial tram car hanging precariously from one cable 80 feet in the air. The car had been cut nearly in half when the tram derailed and the other cable cut through the roof of the car. An estimated 17 tons of force pinned 12 passengers to the floor of the tram. One side of the car had been torn open, exposing passengers to a howling wind and snowstorm a few hundred feet from the top of High Camp at Squaw Valley, Calif. Seventy passengers from the other car on the same lift were left stranded 300 feet in the air by the accident. It necessitated two simultaneous 11-hour rescues at night. Jim Mott, Squaw Valley Patrol leader, directed the entire operation by radio while standing at the five-foot opening of the damaged tram car with his back exposed to the blizzard and the 80-foot drop, giving the final check for frostbite, shock, and rigging to each person, and then helping them out of the car on the rope evacuation to safety.

2. The rescue of 12 skiers by the Vail Ski Patrol from the Vail gondolas after the tragic accident of March 26, 1976. One member of the Ski Patrol climbed the lift cable, over 100 feet in the air, to secure the dangling gondola to the cable. The Ski Patrol evacuated the

passengers to safety by ropes, administered first aid to nine seriously injured survivors of the fallen gondolas and arranged helicopter evacuation to Denver hospitals. They then evacuated 215 passengers hanging from 100 to 250 feet in the air in the stranded gondolas in seven-hour rescue.

3. The rescue of a 7-year-old girl, who slipped from a ski lift and was caught by her parka by her father, 25 feet in the air, at Homewood Ski Area, Calif., in 1973. Ski Patrollers Craig Ellis and Helmut Bechtle, hearing the cries for help, skied under the lift in time to catch the girl, still wearing her skis, as she slipped from her father's grasp. Anything less than instantaneous action by the Patrollers would have resulted in serious injury, or death, for the girl, who was uninjured.

4. The rescue by Ski Patroller Rollin Randall during a training exercise at June Mountain, California, on March 4, 1973. When the trainees fell in difficult skiing conditions on new powder over broken crust and the rescue sled accelerated free, straight down the mountain (Carson Run, ranked as the seventh steepest ski run in the U.S.), Randall skate-skied in pursuit, catching the sled with a headlong dive and bulldogging it in an arc to avoid trees, finally bringing it to a stop, with no injuries. Said one reporter: "Few of us through life ever get to witness such an act of courage and decision."

5. The rescue by the Snowbird Ski Patrol in 1971 of a 19-year-old from an avalanche that released 3½ hours after normal avalance control had been conducted. He was buried in 2½ feet of tightly packed snow. The Ski Patrol organized several probe lines, but the first probe did not find the skier. Another line was formed. An hour had elapsed since the slide, and hope that the boy was still alive had faded. This time, the probe

located the boy. He was blue because of a lack of oxygen, but his pulse was strong. First mouth-to-mouth resuscitation, then oxygen, revived him. He said he could hear the rescuers working over him the first time and shouted as loud as he could, but he was not heard, and he figured his chance was gone.

6. The rescue of a man and his wife by the Mt. Pilchuck (Wash.) Ski Patrol in 1971. The couple was swept down a 200-foot cliff and a 100-foot slope when a crevice collapsed, burying the husband (except for one hand) and injuring both skiers. The woman dug her husband out with her hands and her ski pole. After climbing two miles in dangerous avalanche-hazard snow, the Ski Patrollers administered first aid to the couple for multiple injuries and for shock. They then descended the mountain over cliffs, necessitating several delays because of avalanche hazard over ⅓ of a mile, followed by one mile of breakable crust. The rescue, mostly at night, took 6½ hours.

7. The rescue by Ski Patrollers Owen Henry and William Nash of a 16-year-old boy on Bolton Mountain, Vt., in 1970. The boy had collapsed on a snowshoe trek when he and his two companions became lost in snow, sinking to their armpits with each step. Henry and Nash dragged a rescue sled a mile uphill until the steepness was too great to pull the sled farther. They scrambled the last 1,000 feet and found the boy semiconscious and incoherent. They administered first aid, wrapped him in a blanket, dragged him to the sled, then pulled the sled a mile to a waiting snow cat and medical attention. The entire rescue took place in waist-deep snow.

8. The rescue of a young girl at Mammoth Mountain, Calif., in 1969. She had slipped returning from a steep canyon overlook, falling 100 feet down the canyon

wall, and was bleeding and unconscious, with a fractured skull. Ski Patroller Larry Nye, realizing time was critical, ran and slid down the same slope without equipment. Reaching her, Nye treated her injuries and stopped the bleeding with his own clothing, then assisted and directed her removal from the canyon and continued to administer first aid in the ambulance until they reached Mammoth Mountain Hospital.

9. The October 12, 1958 rescue by Ski Patrollers Hart Axley and Ken Wright and Boy Scouts Ric Marcus and Edgar Stratton of a 14-year-old Boy Scout who had fallen 20 feet in a rock slide just below the Continental Divide above Lake Isabelle in Colorado. The boy sustained critical head and internal injuries, and fractures of the back, ribs, pelvis, and one leg, landing in a small pool of ice cold water, causing near hypothermia, above cliffs that made him inaccessible to his companions and leaders. Ski Patrollers Axley and Wright and Scouts Marcus and Stratton improvised a stretcher, splint, and bandages from available clothing and scrub brush from the timberline, and inched the boy down cliffs and scree slopes in a five-hour, 10-mile rescue trail in darkness.

10. The rescue of 30 people buried in cars by a surprise June blizzard at 11,000 feet in Beartooth Pass, California, in 1947. Percy Bliss and Dick Green carried over 100 pounds of food, coffee, and clothing 20 miles up the pass through blinding snow in 10-degree temperatures and high winds. They brought out five people at a time, making six trips in the two-day rescue operation.

SOURCE: Hart Axley of National Ski Patrol System, Inc.

XI

By a Nose

Joe Hirsch's 10 Handsomest Horses

Executive columnist for the *Daily Racing Form*, Joe Hirsch has been following horses as a writer for 30 years. He has seen every Triple Crown race for a quarter of a century and is at home at most of the leading tracks in the United States, Canada, France, England, and Ireland. He was first president of the National Turf Writers Assn. He knows good bloodlines when he sees them, which is somewhat akin to Joe Namath as a connoisseur of women. It happens that Joe Namath and Joe Hirsch used to be roommates.

1. Secretariat—The perfect horse. A beau ideal from every standpoint of conformation.
2. Gen. Duke—The best-balanced horse I've ever seen and one of the greatest until his tragic demise.
3. Mongo—He glittered and gleamed with good health.
4. Majestic Prince—Robust, handsome and muscular. Red as a copper penny.

5. Ruffian—The only filly to make as impressive an appearance as her immense talent.

6. Diablo—If a horse was ever going to be a film star, he would fill the bill.

7. Honest Pleasure—You looked at him and knew he was something special.

8. Lucky Debonair—Dashing in appearance, he was an equine Valentino.

9. Alydar—Rugged and ready. The Charles Bronson of horses.

10. Nashua—The soundest horse who ever lived. You couldn't hurt him with a baseball bat.

Jim Bolus' 10 Worst Kentucky Derby Starters

Jim Bolus of the *Louisville Times,* a former publicity director for Churchill Downs, is author of *Run for the Roses,* a history of the Kentucky Derby. He was a staff writer for the *Louisville Courier-Journal* and, with Billy Reed, won a National Headliners Award and Sigma Delta Chi Distinguished Service Award in 1972 for investigative stories on the Kentucky thoroughbred industry. He has witnessed every "Run for the Roses" since 1959.

1. Senacas Coin (pulled up, 1949)—Indisputably the worst horse ever to run in the Derby, this nag was ridden by Jimmy Duff, who encountered a newsman in the paddock after the race and asked: "Who win?" It was a logical question, since Senacas Coin had pulled up nearly a quarter of a mile behind the victorious Ponder. The Derby was no fluke for Senacas Coin, who started 53 times in his career. He lost 52.

2. Frank Bird (last in 1908)—Never close in six lifetime starts, three of which resulted in last-place finishes for

Secretariat won the Triple Crown in 1973.   *Dick Martin*

this creature. Those six races drew a total of 59 starters. Only six finished behind Frank Bird.

3. Orlandwick (last in 1907)—He did manage to win
   twice in 30 starts, but he once proved beyond a shadow
   of a doubt that he was a first-rate dog—he was one of
   those who finished behind Frank Bird.

4. Pravus (last in 1923)—Twenty career starts and never
   a winner. Wonder if he ever stopped to nibble on cans
   in the post parade.

5. Dick O'Hara (last in 1930)—Fifteen starts, one victory
   and seven last-place finishes.

6. Saigon Warrior (last in 1971)—Even though he finished 72¼ lengths back, it's not true that they needed
   lanterns to find Saigon Warrior when he finally
   dragged himself home. They were using flashlights.

7. Fourulla (next-to-last in 1971)—Beaten by 58¼
   lengths. Flashlights for him, too.

8. Layson (third in 1905)—How could a third-place fin-
   isher be so bad? Easy. There were only three starters.
   Layson's career produced good news and bad news.
   The good: He won three times. The bad: He lost 88.

9. Broadway Limited (also-ran in 1930)—Sold for $65,000
   as a yearling. Not only did he fail to win in nine career
   starts, he never finished in the money and didn't even
   earn the first penny. An overpriced bum.

10. Rae Jet (last in 1969)—His Derby trainer, Jimmy Cos-
    don, once said this horse (horse?) had received more
    publicity than Frank Sinatra. Cosdon never got around
    to answering one question: Could Rae Jet outrun
    Sinatra?

Delvin Miller's 5 Greatest Trotters and 5 Greatest Pacers

Delvin Miller, harness racing's good-will ambassador, has
done it all in four decades in the sport—driver, trainer,

breeder, owner, selector of yearlings, and race track president. As a driver, he has had almost 2,000 winners and almost $9 million in earnings and has won all of the sport's major races.

TROTTERS

1. Greyhound
2. Scott Frost
3. Nevele Pride
4. Goldsmith Maid
5. Green Speed

PACERS

1. Dan Patch
2. Calumet Evelyn
3. Albatross
4. Single G
5. Bret Hanover

Dan Patch was a household name in the early 1900s. *UPI*

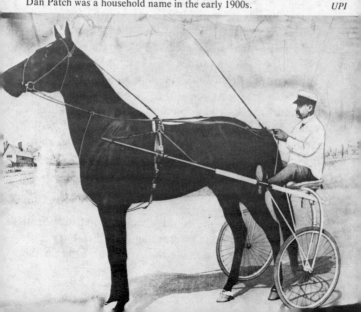

Miller says: "This is a tough assignment. The last two are always hardest to pick. Calumet Evelyn took a record on trot and pace in the same week and was a great mare."

Lou Miller's 12 Most Fascinating Harness Horses

Lou (no relation to Delvin) Miller covered a variety of sports for the *New York World-Telegram and Sun* from 1933 until its death in 1966. He is an ex-hurdler who drove and trained harness horses for a decade at New York's Roosevelt and Yonkers raceways. A one-man humane society, he has saved many a horse from a butcher's block-finish by coming up in the nick of time with necessary funds to edge the butchers. He is communications director for New York City Off Track Betting Corporation.

1. Kate—The Phidippides of trotters. In 1850 she pulled a sulky with John F. Purdy aboard 100 miles in nine hours, 49 minutes, 15 seconds around the Centerville Course on Long Island, and then died.
2. Goldsmith Maid—The creaking old mare who, at age 17 in 1874 in Boston, drew driver Budd Doble to a new world trotting record of 2:14. This was in an era when harness horses were allowed to go only fast enough to win and when they had to pull wagons or high-wheeled sulkies and trot or pace three to six heats before deciding the winner of a race. Nowadays the rules retire horses after age 14. Goldie began cracking world records at 14 and lowered the standard eight times, including five universal bests at 17.
3. Une de Mai of France—She didn't have enough quick speed to sprint around Nevele Pride and get to the rail in the 1969 Roosevelt International at Westbury, L.I. Despite being kept outside the American kingpin the

entire 1½ miles, she pulled driver Jean Rene Gougeon to victory. This was shortly before Pride went on to the current world trotting record of 1:54.4.

4. Greyhound—He didn't look like much as a yearling in 1933 when purchased for a paltry $900. In 1938 at Lexington, Ky., his gigantic trotting strides carried him and S.F. Palin to a 1:55¼ all-time mark that lasted 31 years, until Nevele Pride sliced it.

5. Nevele Pride—Set the all-time trot standard of 1:54.4 in 1969 at Indianapolis, with Stanley Dancer sulky-sitting. This was despite a nasty temper that kept him preoccupied with trying to bite and kick his driver, trainer, and any unsuspecting visitors.

6. Dan Patch—He drew 70,000 onlookers to an exhibition race in Allentown, Pa., in 1905. There were Dan Patch dances, cigars, pillow cases, scarfs, coaster wagons, hobby horses. He didn't use hobbles around his legs to keep him pacing, but he set the world record of 1:55¼ in 1905, with H.C. Hersey driving at Lexington, Ky.

7. John R. Gentry—In his sixth race of the day at Portland, Me., in 1896, he set the universal standard of 2:00½ with Jay Andrews piloting.

8. Sleepy Tom—A completely blind pacer, he set the world mark of 2:12½ in 1879 in Chicago, guided by the voice of his driver, S.C. Phillips.

9. Adios Harry—He had to have two head poles, one on each side of his neck, to keep him steering straight. He also needed hobbles and knee- and leg-boots to keep him from kicking chunks out of his underpinning. Still he equaled Billy Direct's world record of 1:55 in 1955 at Vernon with comparatively inexperienced Luther Lyons driving and training him.

10. Steady Star, Jamin, and Hairos in a dead heat—Steady

12. Star never won much acclaim in regular races. Never-

theless, this free-legged pacer set the 1:52 best ever mark in 1971 in a time trial at age four at Lexington with Joe O'Brien driving.

Jamin of France, wearing red ear muffs and on a diet of artichokes, carried Jean Riaud to victory in the first Roosevelt International in 1959.

Hairos II of Holland, wearing his front shoes turned backwards but going forward, pulled 300-pound Willie Geersen two-wide the entire 1¼ mile to win the second Roosevelt International before a record 54,000.

XII

Here's to the Losers

16 Famous Injuries That Changed the Course of Sports History

1. BABE RUTH'S BELLYACHE

It was called "the bellyache heard around the world," by writer W.O. McGeehan. The attack came during the spring of 1925, and on April 17, surgery was performed. Ruth returned to the lineup on June 1, which proved to be a mistake. Babe never fully recovered. He played in only 98 games, batting .290 (88 points less than the previous year) and hitting 25 homers (21 less than the previous year). The Yankees, who had finished first three times and second once in the preceding four seasons, dropped to seventh in 1925.

2. WALLY PIPP'S HEADACHE

A simple headache sidelined the veteran first baseman of the New York Yankees on June 1, 1925. He was replaced by a young man named Lou Gehrig, who started that game and began a streak of playing in 2,130 consecutive games, a record.

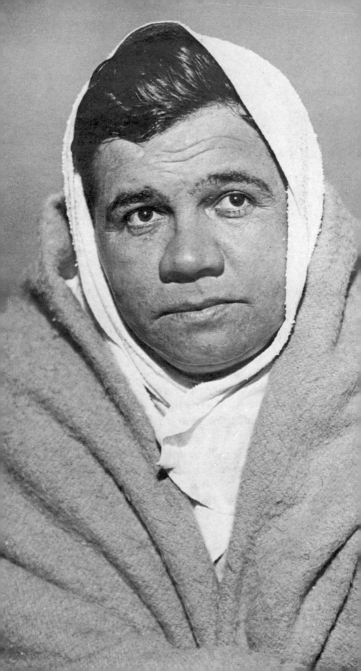

3. GEORGE SHAW'S BROKEN LEG

It happened on October 21, 1956, in a game between the Baltimore Colts and Chicago Bears. Shaw, the Colts' regular quarterback, was piled up by three huge Bear linemen, breaking his leg. He was replaced by a young man who had been cut by the Pittsburgh Steelers. Once he got his chance, Johnny Unitas became one of the greatest quarterbacks in the history of pro football.

4. JOE DiMAGGIO'S HEEL

A bone spur in his right heel caused the great DiMaggio to miss the first 65 games of the 1949 season. He returned on June 28 and, in a three-game series with the Boston Red Sox, slugged four homers and drove in nine runs as the Yankees swept the series. He played in 76 games, batting .346 with 14 homers and 67 RBI and led the Yankees to the first of their record five consecutive world championships. However, it was DiMaggio's heel problem that caused him to retire, prematurely, after the 1951 season.

5. STAN MUSIAL'S INJURED SHOULDER

In 1940, Musial was a young player for the Daytona Beach Islanders, an outstanding prospect as both a pitcher and an outfielder. Pitching seemed to be his forte, until he fell in the outfield and injured his left shoulder, finishing him as a pitcher. But he concentrated on hitting, and became one of the great hitters of all time, winning seven National League batting titles, finishing his career with 3,630 hits and a lifetime batting average of .331.

6. MUHAMMAD ALI'S HERNIA

Scheduled to make the first defense of his heavyweight title against the tough Sonny Liston in Boston, Ali sustained a

Babe Ruth's bellyaches and pains were always front-page news.   *UPI*

hernia on the eve of the fight. It came during Ali's problems with the Army and the rematch was shifted several times, finally winding up in Lewiston, Me. The six months' delay worked to the disadvantage of the aging Liston, who was KOd in a controversial and suspicious fight.

7. DIZZY DEAN'S TOE

In the 1937 All-Star Game, Dean was struck on the right foot by a line drive off the bat of Earl Averill. Dean retired from the game with a broken toe. When he tried to come back too soon from the injury, he threw with an unnatural motion that caused an arm injury. He finished with a 13–10 record that season after winning 102 games in the four preceding years. In the next three years, he won only 16 games and soon was out of baseball.

8. WILLIS REED'S HIP

Driving for the basket midway in game No. 5 of the 1969–70 NBA championship playoffs against the Los Angeles Lakers, Reed fell to the floor and writhed in pain. He was badly hurt, and when he left the game, it seemed he would play no more basketball that year. With him went the New York Knicks' chances of winning their first world championship in their 24-year history. But several nights later, in game No. 7, Reed courageously returned. He played only 27 minutes, scored only four points, grabbed only three rebounds, but his grit, determination, and courage gave the Knicks the impetus to win the climactic seventh game and the title.

9. PETE REISER'S CONCUSSION

A brilliant career was dramatically curtailed when Reiser kept slamming into outfield walls while chasing fly balls. He led the National League in batting as a rookie with a .343 average for the Brooklyn Dodgers in 1942 and was heralded as a potential Hall of Famer. He never reached that pinnacle as a result of injuries, although he played 10 years in the major leagues with a .295 lifetime batting average.

10. BOBBY THOMSON'S BROKEN ANKLE

Thomson broke his ankle in spring training, 1954. He forced the Milwaukee Braves to reach down to their minor league farm club in Savannah for a skinny, young outfielder. His name was Hank Aaron and he became the greatest home run hitter in baseball history.

11. BUSTER MATHIS' BROKEN FINGER

A training injury sidelined Mathis, who was to represent the United States as a heavyweight in the 1964 Olympics in Tokyo. He was replaced by an alternate, Joe Frazier, who won the Olympic title, then went on to become the heavyweight champion of the world.

12. CHARLEY GELBERT'S LEG INJURY

A hunting accident caused the leg injury that kept Gelbert out of the 1933 and 1934 seasons. Desperate for a shortstop to replace Gelbert, the St. Louis Cardinals purchased a little-used shortstop from the Cincinnati Reds. His name was Leo Durocher and he became a vital part of the Gashouse Gang, and, later, one of the most colorful, controversial, and successful managers in the game.

13. HOIST THE FLAG'S LEG

An injury to this colt, shortly before the 1971 Kentucky Derby, scratched him from the big race. He would have been a solid 1–5 favorite and the likely winner. In his absence, an unheralded colt from Venezuela named Cannonero II won the race. He was so lightly regarded, he was included in the "field." As a solo entry, he would have been at least 100-to-one. His victory was one of the most dramatic and popular in Derby history.

14. HERB SCORE'S FACE

A line drive off the bat of Gil McDougald struck Score in the face and cut short a brilliant career. Score had won 36 games in his first two big league seasons, leading the American League in strikeouts both years with 245 and 263. After the injury, he won only 17 games in five seasons.

15. EDDIE WAITKUS' GUNSHOT WOUND

Waitkus had been traded by the Chicago Cubs to the Philadelphia Phillies, for whom he was having a good year in 1949. The season was one-third over when he was shot in the stomach by a deranged female fan. It finished him for the season, but he recovered to have three productive years for the Phillies, helping them win the 1950 National League championship.

16. MONTY STRATTON'S LEG

A promising pitching career was halted when the Chicago White Sox pitcher lost his leg by a self-inflicted gunshot wound during a hunting accident in 1938. This courageous man actually returned to the minor leagues, pitching with an artificial leg, but never pitched again in the major leagues.

15 Great Upsets

1. John Thomas' defeat by Russian Robert Shavlakadze in the 1960 Olympics in Rome after the medal had all but been awarded to the American.
2. James J. Braddock's victory over Max Baer in 1935 to win the world heavyweight championship. Braddock, considered washed up at 30, was a 10–1 underdog, but

his victory earned him the nickname "Cinderella Man."

3. The New York Jets' 16–7 victory over the Baltimore Colts in Super Bowl III. The Colts were 18-point favorites, but Joe Namath "guaranteed" victory in a pregame boast, then made it stand up as the Jets became the first team from the upstart American Football League to beat an NFL team in the big one.

4. The upset of the great Man O' War, an 11–20 favorite, by a horse aptly named Upset, an 8–1 choice, in the Sanford Stakes at Saratoga Springs in 1919.

5. A World Series victory in 1969 by the New York Mets over the Baltimore Orioles. The Orioles had won the first game, but the Mets came back to win the next four. An expansion team, the Mets were formed in 1962. In 1968, they finished in ninth place in the National League, 24 games out of first.

6. The victory of Cassius Clay (Muhammad Ali) over seemingly indestructible Sonny Liston for the heavyweight championship in Miami Beach in 1964. Liston, a 7–1 favorite, failed to come out for the seventh round.

7. The surprise victory of unknown Jack Fleck over the great Ben Hogan in the 1955 United States Open in San Francisco. Fleck had never finished higher than fifth on the pro tour. Hogan had won the Open four times in a spectacular career.

8. Thor Hanover, 70–1, beating 3–10 favorite Adora's Dream to win the $169,000 Messenger Stakes at Roosevelt Raceway in 1962.

9. Unheralded Notre Dame, playing in the East for the first time, used a secret weapon—the forward passing of Gus Dorais—to beat Army, 35–10, and burst upon the national college football scene in 1913.

10. Leon Spinks, a 6–1 underdog fighting only his eighth

Joe Namath and the Jets shook the football world with their upset of the Colts in the Super Bowl.

Ken Regan

pro fight, beating Muhammad Ali in 1978 to win the world heavyweight title.

11. George Robson, a virtual unknown, winning the 1946 Indianapolis 500 from a field that included auto racing legends Ralph Hepburn, Rex Mays, Tony Bettenhausen, and Sam Hanks.

12. The 7-0 victory by Ivy League Columbia over mighty Stanford in the 1934 Rose Bowl.

13. Howard Ehmke, 35 years old, getting the surprise call to be the opening-game pitcher for the Philadelphia A's against the Chicago Cubs in the 1929 World Series. Ehmke, who had won only seven games all season, beat the Cubs, 3-1, striking out a record 13 batters, and the A's won the Series in five games.

14. The Chicago Black Hawks, disorganized all season, beating the strong Toronto Maple Leafs to win the 1938 Stanley Cup.

15. City College, 17-5 during the regular season, beating top-ranked Bradley in both the NIT and NCAA tournaments in 1950 to stand as the only team in college basketball history to win both major events in the same year.

Bill Libby's 10 Most Memorable Losers

Bill Libby has written more than 50 books, including James Roosevelt's *My Parents: A Different View,* Deacon Jones' *Life in the Pit,* and John Roseboro's *Glory Days With the Dodgers.* His list is from a book, *The Losers,* which is unpublished "because it was considered 'downbeat.' But most of us are losers in life and I have found material closest to life in losers' dressing rooms and done my best and best-received stories on losers." His most memorable is a list limited to winners who wound up losers in some way:

1. Eddie Sachs—No one I have known wanted anything more than Eddie wanted to win the Indianapolis 500. But when a tire went bad in the 1961 race, he gave up the lead in the last laps rather than risk his life. But in the 1964 race, he lost his life, anyway.

2. Davey Moore—The world featherweight champion lost not only his title but his life in a 1963 bout against Sugar Ramos in Dodger Stadium that typifies the hard life, and sometimes death, of the professional fighter.

3. Ted Horn—The great racer finished second, third, or fourth nine straight years without ever winning the Indianapolis 500, and his death, in a race in Illinois in 1948, typifies the daring and deaths of such great drivers as Tony Bettenhausen, Rex Mays, and others who never won "the big one" in this cruelest sport.

4. Ralph Branca—Death is one way for a loser to lose, but sometimes it may be harder to live with defeat. One pitch, which the New York Giants' Bobby Thomson hit for a home run in the famous 1951 playoff game against the Brooklyn Dodgers, labeled Branca a loser forever and landed him alongside the luckless Fred Merkle, Johnny Pesky, Mickey Owen, Ernie Lombardi and, most recently, Garry Maddox, and so many more who made mistakes at the worst time.

5. 1951 Dodgers, 1964 Phillies, 1978 Red Sox—And all the other teams in sports that lost large leads down the stretch in any season, leaving their players to live the rest of their lives with the label "choke-ups."

The agony of defeat: Ralph Branca *(back to camera)* with Cookie Lavagetto after the fatal home run pitch. *Barney Stein/N.Y. Post*

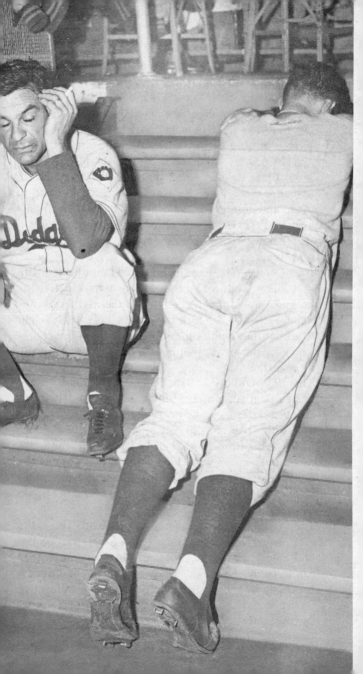

6. The Red Sox, who have not won a World Series since 1918, the White Sox, since 1917, the Cubs, since 1908, the Phillies, since "never," and all those teams in sports who never once have taken the title. There is no law that says their time will not come some day.

7. Jerry West and Elgin Baylor—And the rest of the Los Angeles Lakers, who reached the NBA playoff finals seven times in nine years, the final game four times, and lost every time. No team ever came so close so often and lost every time. When the Lakers finally won, in 1972, the newly retired Baylor stood silently in the shadows, while West admitted he did not know how to act.

8. Billy Conn—Who had the great Joe Louis beaten with a brilliant and courageous boxing effort before he became overconfident, went for the KO, and was knocked out in the 13th round of a 1941 heavyweight title bout that typifies the efforts of so many underdogs who have the great upset in their hands, then see it slip away at the last.

9. The 1938 Duke Football Team—Which had an un-beaten, untied, unscored-upon season until a third-string quarterback, Doyle Nave, threw a touchdown pass with 41 seconds to play to give USC a 7-3 victory in the 1939 Rose Bowl. I locked myself in the bath-room and wept. I was 11 years old. I don't know why Duke was my team, but its loss was mine and typifies all the losses suffered by all the boys, who never again will root as hard for their teams.

10. The Coaches—"The Old Grey Fox" is dead. This is the most degraded of professions. I feel for all the coaches and managers who worry about losing so much, they can't enjoy winning; who must endure endless pressure; who bear the blame for all the failures of their players; and who are fired so freely, so carelessly, so constantly.

Honorable Mention: Every player and every team who ever lost a playoff, who ever lost their one chance at a championship. Every "championship player," who never played on a championship team. A Jim Ryun or a Ron Clarke, who won everything but the Olympics, who typify the athletes, such as Bob Feller, who beat everyone, but never won the big one. A Harvey Haddix, who lost a "perfect game" in the 13th inning because his team couldn't score a run for him. A Clay Kirby, who lost a no-hitter because his manager pinch-hit for him in an effort to win one more game for a team that hadn't won many games rather than reward a player who performed so valiantly, or the fans who rooted so fruitlessly. And all the "other chances" that never came. Roy Riegels and all the rest who ran the wrong way or did the wrong thing at the wrong time and had to live with being reminded of it the rest of their lives.

Otis Elevator's 10 Most Up and Down Boxers

1. Christy Williams, knocked down 42 times in a 17-round fight with Battling Nelson on Dec. 26, 1902. Nelson was knocked down 7 times.
2. Jack Havlin, knocked down 42 times in a 29-round fight with Tommy Warren on Sept. 25, 1888.
3. Miguel Ferrara, knocked down 36 times in five rounds in a fight against Vittorio Campolo in Buenos Aires on Sept. 7, 1925.
4. Leach Cross, knocked down 32 times in 41 rounds by Dick Hyland in their fight on June 25, 1909.
5. Danny Webster, knocked down 27 times in 13 rounds in a fight with Mexican Joe Rivers, Jan. 14, 1911.
6. Joe Jeannette, knocked down 27 times by Sam McVey, who was down 11 times, in their 49-round fight on April 17, 1909, in Paris, France.

7. Hal Murray, down 23 times in five rounds against Harry Blitman on Dec. 28, 1931.

8. Jock Porter, down 21 times in seven rounds in a fight against Olle Tandberg in Stockholm on Jan. 8, 1948.

9. Jose DeMedina, knocked down 21 times by Jimmy Jennette in their 10-round fight on Nov. 18, 1946.

10. Jim Merritt, knocked down 20 times by Maxie Doyle, who was down 3 times, in their 10-round fight on Nov. 24, 1941.

EDITOR'S NOTE: New York, and other states, adopted a rule on Feb. 27, 1957, which automatically stops a fight when one fighter has been knocked down 3 times in one round. The rule is waived for championship fights and the record for most knockdowns in a title fight is 14, Danny Sullivan being floored that many times in 10 rounds in his unsuccessful attempt to win the world bantamweight championship from Vic Toweel in Johannesburg, South Africa, on Dec. 2, 1950.

SOURCE: *The Ring Boxing Encyclopedia and Record Book* (The Ring Book Shop).

12 Famous Sports Boners

1. FRED MERKLE

In a tense pennant race between the Chicago Cubs and New York Giants, the two clubs met on September 23, 1908. The score was tied, 2–2, in the last of the ninth with two out and Giant runners on first and third, when Al Bridwell singled in what appeared to be the winning run. Fred Merkle, a 19-year-old substitute first baseman, was the runner on first, and when Bridwell's hit landed safely in the outfield, Merkle peeled off and raced into the clubhouse without touching second base, a common practice of the day. Chicago second baseman Johnny Evers called for the ball, stepped on second and invoked a seldom-used rule. Umpire Hank O'Day called Merkle out, disallowing the winning run. A riot ensued and the game could not continue. It was decided to replay the game after the season, if necessary. It became necessary when the Cubs and Giants finished with identical records of 98–53. But Chicago won the playoff and the pennant and Merkle's boner cost the Giants a pennant. For the rest of his 16-year career, he was called "Bonehead" Merkle.

2. WRONG-WAY RIEGELS

It happened in the 1929 Rose Bowl game between Georgia Tech and California. Georgia Tech, heavily favored but experiencing difficulty against a tough California team, had the ball on its 25-yard line early in the second quarter. Tailback Stumpy Thomason was hit as he drove off left tackle, the jarring tackle knocking the ball from his grasp. The ball landed on the ground and was scooped up by California center Roy Riegels, who began running toward the Georgia Tech goal line. To avoid two tacklers, Riegels made a horseshoe turn, losing his bearings. He began running in the wrong direction, toward the California goal line, with teammate Barney Lom in pursuit, trying to head off Riegels. Lom finally grabbed Riegels' arm, stopping him one yard from the goal line. On the next play, California punted, but the ball was blocked into the end zone for a safety, which proved to be the margin of Georgia Tech's 8–7 victory.

3. WRONG-WAY MARSHALL

It was 35 years after Riegels' boner that Minnesota Viking tackle Jim Marshall experienced the same embarrassing fate. In a game against the San Francisco 49ers, Marshall picked up a ball fumbled by 49er quarterback Billy Kilmer and took off for the goal line—the wrong one. He raced 66 yards into the end zone, and not until he got there did he realize his mistake. Instead of scoring six points for the Vikings, he scored two for the 49ers, but lived down his mistake by playing better than ever in Minnesota's 27-22 victory.

4. MICKEY OWEN'S DROPPED STRIKE

The Brooklyn Dodgers, who had never won a world championship, seemed to have their hated rivals, the New York Yankees, on the run in the 1941 Series. The Yankees led, two games to one, but the Dodgers were one strike away from wrapping up game No. 4. The Dodgers led, 4-3, with two out and nobody on base in the ninth. Relief pitcher Hugh Casey got two strikes on Tommy Henrich, then fired a pitch that dipped down and in. Henrich swung and missed for strike three . . . but the ball sailed past catcher Owen and Henrich reached base safely. The powerful Yankees capitalized on the goof, striking for four runs and a 7-4 victory, then won the following day to win the Series, four games to one.

5. THE LONG COUNT

Eager to win the heavyweight championship he had lost to Gene Tunney a year before, Jack Dempsey was a tiger in the ring at Soldier Field, Chicago, on Sept. 22, 1927. In the seventh round, Dempsey swarmed all over Tunney, knocking him down with a flurry of punches so powerful it seemed they would keep Tunney down for the count. But mysteriously, Dempsey hovered over the fallen Tunney instead of complying with a new rule and heading for a neutral corner. Dempsey was frozen, and referee Jack Barry's attempts to get him to his corner were fruitless. Finally, for what seemed to be several critical seconds, Dempsey moved to the corner and Barry began his count. Some say Dempsey wasted as many as eight seconds. In any case, the extra time permitted Tunney's head to clear and he rose just as Barry was about to count 10. Given a reprieve, Tunney went on to win the fight by a decision, and only Dempsey's boner allowed Tunney to retain his heavyweight title.

6. CLEM McCARTHY'S CALL

The famed announcer pulled the biggest rock of his distinguished career in the 1947 running of the Preakness Stakes. To a national radio audience, he announced that Faultless had won the race when, in reality, the winner was Jet Pilot.

7. TOMMY LEWIS' TACKLE

It happened in the 1954 Cotton Bowl game between Alabama and Rice. Fullback Lewis had given an underdog Alabama team its first touchdown, but the Crimson Tide trailed, 7–6, late in the first half when Rice halfback Dicky Moegle took off from his 5-yard line. He had outrun the Alabama secondary and was on his way to a 95-yard touchdown run that would have given Rice a commanding lead. He was racing past the Alabama bench, right before the eyes of a dejected and intense Tommy Lewis. Suddenly, Lewis sprang from the bench and brought Moegle down on the 38-yard line with a perfect tackle. Quickly, he returned to the bench, but the referee had spotted the infraction, disallowed the tackle and awarded the touchdown to Moegle. Alabama went on to a 28–6 victory. "I guess I'm too full of Alabama," Lewis later explained. "He just ran too close. I didn't know what I was doing. After I pulled him down, I jumped up and got back on the bench and kept telling myself: 'I didn't do it, I didn't do it.' But I knew I did."

8. SNODGRASS' MUFF

The 1912 World Series was a tense, tight duel between the New York Giants and Boston Red Sox. After six games, the Series was tied, three games apiece. After nine innings of the seventh game, the score was tied 1-1. The Giants scored a run in the top of the 10th. Pinch-hitter Clyde Engle led off the Boston 10th with a lazy fly to center field. The ball slipped through the hands of Giant centerfielder Fred Snodgrass for a two-base error, paving the way for the Red Sox to score two runs to win the game, 3-2, and the Series, four games to three. Snodgrass was the goat, his error going down in history as "the $30,000 muff," that sum being the difference between the winning and losing team's Series share.

9. DARTMOUTH'S TWELFTH MAN

It happened in the snow-splattered game between Dartmouth and Princeton for the 1935 Ivy League championship. Both teams were undefeated, but on this day Princeton clearly displayed its superiority. Princeton was on its way to a 26-6 victory when, late in the fourth period, as the Dartmouth defense lined up to stop another Princeton drive, a spectator dashed onto the field and lined up between Dartmouth tackle Dave Camerer and guard Joe Handrahan. "Kill those Princeton guys," he shouted, then leaped across the line, fell on his face and was pummeled by Princeton players. Policemen escorted the 12th man from the field and he disappeared, his identity and his motivation never to be revealed.

10. JOHNNY PESKY'S DELAY

The St. Louis Cardinals and Boston Red Sox were tied, 3-3 in games and 3-3 in runs in the eighth inning of the climactic seventh game of the 1946 World Series. Enos Slaughter led off the bottom of the 8th with a single and, two outs later, was still on first when Harry Walker lined a single to left center. Expecting Slaughter to stop at second, Sox shortstop Pesky took the throw from the outfield and held the ball for a critical split-second while Slaughter charged around third and kept right on going home. Pesky's delay enabled Slaughter to dash home with the winning run in the final game of the Series. That winter, Pesky relates, he was home in Seattle watching a football game. The University of Washington halfbacks were plagued with fumbles. Finally, a loudmouthed fan shouted a suggestion. "Give the ball to Pesky," he said. "He'll hold on to it."

11. THE FIFTH DOWN

Underdog Dartmouth had apparently held heavily favored Cornell deep in Dartmouth territory for a 3–0 victory in their 1940 meeting. With nine seconds left, a desperation pass on fourth down was batted down and the ball went over to Dartmouth. Or did it? A delay-of-game penalty prior to the pass had confused referee Red Friesell, and linesman Joe McKenny convinced him that the pass had come on third down, not fourth. Friesell gave the ball to Cornell and the Raiders scored the "winning" touchdown as time ran out. In reviewing the film, Friesell discovered his error, that Cornell had an extra down and that Dartmouth should be declared the winner. He advised Commissioner Asa Bushnell of the Eastern Collegiate Athletic Association of the error, but Bushnell ruled that once a game is over, officials have no authority to change the score. The victory remained Cornell's. However, Cornell coach Carl Snavely believed the only honorable solution was to concede the game to Dartmouth. He did so in a wire to Dartmouth coach Earl "Red" Blaik, and Cornell suffered its first defeat in three years.

12. WILLIE SHOEMAKER'S MISJUDGMENT

Charging through the stretch of the 1957 Kentucky Derby, jockey Shoemaker drove Gallant Man to the lead, head-and-head with Iron Liege. It seemed Gallant Man would open up a lead and win the Run for the Roses. But at the 16th pole, Shoemaker stood up in his saddle. He had misjudged the finish line and stood up, thinking the race was over and he was the winner. Shoemaker quickly discovered his error and dropped down in his seat. But the split-second hesitation was enough for Iron Liege to regain the lead and win the race by a nose.

Ray Fitzgerald's 27 Baseball Flashes in the Pan

As a sportswriter and columnist for the *Boston Globe* for more than three decades, Ray Fitzgerald is no flash in the pan.

1. Bob "Hurricane" Hazle—Promoted from the minor leagues to the Milwaukee Braves on July 11, 1957, he finished the season batting .403 with seven homers and 27 RBI in 41 games. In 1958, he was batting .179 in 20 games when he was sold to the Tigers, where he batted .241 in 43 games and was released, his entire major league career consisting of two months.

2. Dave Nicholson—Signed by the Baltimore Orioles for $100,000 in 1959, he hit 22 homers in 1963. But in 1,419 major league at-bats, he struck out 573 times, including a record 175 Ks in 1963.

3. Clyde Vollmer—Obtained by the Boston Red Sox in a trade with Washington in July of 1951, his bat won 13 games in the month. But he was traded back to Washington, batted .256 in 1954, and retired.

4. Dale Alexander—Won the American League batting championship with .367 for the Red Sox in 1932. Two years later, at age 30, he was out of baseball.

5. Al Weis—A .215 hitter as a part-time player for the Mets in 1969, he batted .455 in the World Series. The

following year, he got in only 11 games and was released in July.

6. Blondy Ryan—Brash shortstop for the New York
Giants who left the team in 1933 because of a contract
dispute. With the Giants in a hot pennant race, Ryan
reconsidered and sent manager Bill Terry a wire: "We
can't lose, I'm on my way." Helped the Giants win the
pennant and lasted in the majors until 1938, but
nothing he did on the field ever matched his seven-
word telegram.

7. Jim Finigan—Batted .302 for the last-place Philadelphia A's as a rookie in 1954, their last year in Philly.
Then slipped to .255 in 1955 and .216 in 1956, and
went downhill steadily.

8. Frank House—Bonus baby catcher of the Tigers who
was supposed to make Detroit forget Mickey Coch-
rane. He lasted 10 years, but his best average was .259
and his best RBI output was 53.

9. Bobo Holloman—Pitched a no-hitter in his first major
league start as a 29-year-old rookie. He never completed another game and won only two more; his major
league career was brief and ineffective.

10. Karl Spooner—Called up to the Brooklyn Dodgers late
in 1954, he pitched back-to-back shutouts, striking
out 27 men. But a sore arm made him an 8–6 pitcher
in 1955 and he never pitched again.

11. Jim Turner—Won 20 games as a 34-year-old rookie
for the Boston Bees in 1937. He hung on until 1945,
but won only 49 more games.

12. Lou Fette—Won 20 games as a 30-year-old rookie for
the Boston Bees in 1937. Two years later, a sore arm
ended his career.

13. Ron Necciai—Struck out 27 batters in a minor league
game. Called up by the Pirates, his major league
record was 1–6.

14. Billy Rohr—In his first major league start, he pitched 8⅔ innings of no-hit ball against the Yankees in 1967. He won only one more game for Boston, was sold to Cleveland, and quickly faded from view.

15. Clint Hartung—A much-publicized pheenom, the New York Giants could not decide whether to take advantage of his enormous potential as a hitter or a pitcher. Should he become a 30-game winner or a home run champion? He did neither. His lifetime average was .238 with 14 homers. As a pitcher, his career record was 29–29.

16. Al Gionfriddo—Made one of the great catches in World Series history off Joe DiMaggio in 1947. It was the last thing he ever did in the major leagues.

17. Dino Restelli—Hailed as a new Ralph Kiner, he hit 12 homers in 72 games as a Pirate rookie in 1949. The following year, he hit one homer, batted .184, and was out of baseball.

18. Manny Jimenez—Leading the American League in batting at .350 halfway through the 1962 season, he wound up hitting .301 and went steadily downhill.

19. Jim Nash—Won 12, lost one, in 1966 at age 20. Got sore arm, became overweight, and faded from sight.

20. Jerry Walker—At 20, he was the youngest pitcher to win an All-Star Game, in 1959. Stayed in majors through 1964, but never lived up to early promise.

21. Ted Kazanski—$100,000 bonus kid from Hamtramck, Mich., who never fulfilled potential. Six-year average (1953–1958) was .217.

22. Andre Rodgers—Came up after sensational minor league season, but never lived up to billing, despite 11-year career with three teams.

Rookie Clint Hartung reports to the New York Giants' spring training camp in Phoenix in 1947.   *UPI*

23. Paul Pettit—Big bonus kid who was going to be new Grove. Won one game, hurt arm.

24. Rex Barney—Could throw baseball through brick wall, if he could hit wall. Never learned control in 35–31 career, despite no-hitter against Giants.

25. Walt Dropo—Drove in 144 runs in rookie year, was back in Sacramento by July of following season. Returned, however, to have excellent major league career.

26. Wally Bunker—Won 19 games as 19-year-old in '64. Got sore arm in '66, still managed to pitch shutout in Series. Nothing of note thereafter.

27. Dick Wakefield—The answer to Ted Williams, but after one big season, he tapered off, and after coming back from service duty was never much of a player.

Dodger Al Gionfriddo robbed Joe DiMaggio of a home run in the 1947 World Series.   *UPI*

Giorgio Chinaglia (9) has starred for the Cosmos in their championship
seasons.   *Richard Pilling*

XIII

Kicks Heard 'Round the World

Giorgio Chinaglia's 3 Favorite and 1 Worst Soccer Stadiums in the World

Giorgio Chinaglia, formerly of the Italian National team, came to the United States to play for the New York Cosmos of the North American Soccer League and was an instant success—with the fans and on the field. He was greatly responsible for helping the Cosmos win two straight NASL championships and was the league's scoring champion in 1978.

FAVORITE

1. Olympic Stadium in Rome—This is where I played all my home games with my former team, Lazio, and with the Italian National team. In this stadium, I had one of the best experiences in my playing career. The fans would go wild whenever I scored a goal and the atmosphere was always fervent and emotional. The stadium was particularly loud during the annual soccer derby between Lazio and Rome because there were fans for both teams, and, of course, I would receive a few boos

from the opposition. Architecturally, the stadium is beautiful, with a grass field that's a pleasure to play on.

2. Giants Stadium, East Rutherford, N.J.—My favorite place to play and one of the reasons is the structure itself. Physically, it's beautiful (I can't say the same about the artificial turf, but I'm getting used to it). Here the fans are a mixture of American enthusiasts and ethnic fans. I've had very good games in this stadium for the most part. There were a few that upset me, however, usually when we played international teams. The fans at those games were mostly ethnic and did not necessarily cheer for the Cosmos. I usually get both cheers and boos at Giants Stadium, therefore it is always a challenge for me to play there. Booing fans are usually appeased by goal-scoring. Even though I was the top scorer in the league, I think that the New York/New Jersey fans are the most critical.

3. Wembley Stadium, England—One of the European stadiums I enjoy playing in. I was there for one of the most memorable games with the Italian National team when we won, 1–0.

WORST

1. Portland—The surface of the field is in such poor condition that it makes it very difficult to play on.

Kyle Rote Jr.'s NASL All-Star Team (1967–77)

Kyle Rote Jr. is the best-known American-born soccer player, having burst onto the soccer scene by winning the North American Soccer League scoring championship as a rookie with the Dallas Tornado in 1973. He got national attention for himself and his sport by winning television's Superstar competition three times. His all-star team includes only those players from the NASL's first decade, and he picked players on the basis of their play in the league, not on their past performances or reputations.

FIRST TEAM

Goalkeeper—Peter Bonetti, St. Louis Stars
Defender—Franz Beckenbauer, New York Cosmos
Defender—Mike England, Seattle Sounders
Defender—Bobby Smith, Philadelphia Atoms, New York Cosmos
Defender—John Webb, Chicago Sting
Midfielder—Wolfgang Suhnholz, Boston Minutemen, Toronto Metros-Croatia, Las Vegas Quicksilvers, Los Angeles Aztecs, California Surf
Midfielder—Rodney Marsh, Tampa Bay Rowdies
Midfielder—Ilija Mitic, Oakland Clippers, Dallas Tornado, San Jose Earthquake
Forward—Gordon Hill, Chicago Sting
Forward—Giorgio Chinaglia, New York Cosmos
Forward—Pelé, New York Cosmos

SECOND TEAM

Goalkeeper—Ken Cooper, Dallas Tornado
Defender—Ruben Navarro, Cleveland Stokers, Philadelphia Atoms
Defender—Alex Skotarek, Chicago Sting, Tulsa Roughnecks
Defender—Robert Iarusci, Toronto Metros-Croatia, New York Cosmos
Defender—George Ley, Dallas Tornado
Midfielder—Al Trost, St. Louis Stars, California Surf
Midfielder—Alan West, Minnesota Kicks
Midfielder—Antonio Simoes, Boston Minutemen, San Jose Earthquakes
Forward—Derek Smethurst, Tampa Bay Rowdies

Forward—John Kowalik, Chicago Sting
Forward—George Best, Los Angeles Aztecs, Ft. Lauderdale Strikers

SOURCE: *Kyle Rote Jr.'s Complete Book of Soccer,* by Kyle Rote Jr. with Basil Kane (Simon and Schuster).

Phil Woosnam's 10 Greatest Soccer Games

Phil Woosnam is Commissioner of the North American Soccer League.

1. Rochester 2, Dallas 1 (176-minute game, NASL playoffs, 1971)
2. New York 2, Minnesota 1 (shootout "mini-game" in NASL playoffs, 1978)
3. New York 8, Ft. Lauderdale 3 (77,691 crowd, largest in North America, 1977)
4. New York 2, Santos (Brazil) 1 (Pelé farewell game, 1977)
5. England 4, West Germany 2 (overtime, World Cup Final, 1966)
6. Real Madrid 7, Eintracht Frankfurt 3 (European Cup final, 1960)
7. Italy 4, West Germany 3 (overtime, World Cup semifinal, 1970)
8. West Ham 3, at Arsenal, 1 (English League; Woosnam was West Ham player, 1959)
9. Hungary 3, Wales 2 (Friendly International; Woosnam was Wales player, 1961)
10. Atlanta Chiefs 2, Manchester City 1 (second of two exhibitions, 1968)

The legendary Pele scores in his final Cosmos game against Santos in 1977.   *UPI*

Rick Wakeman's All-Time Soccer Team

Rick Wakeman, keyboard wizard of the English rock group "Yes," is a rabid soccer fan, having followed the English Fourth Division club Brentford since his boyhood days and having fulfilled a dream by becoming part owner of the NASL Philadelphia Fury. Says Wakeman: "I selected only those players I have seen more than half-a-dozen times over the last 15 years. For that reason, Pelé does not appear on my list. My team is for a 4-4-2 configuration."

Goal—Gordon Banks, England
Defender—George Cohen, England
Defender—Jimmy Armfield, England
Midfield—Roberto Rivelino, Brazil
Midfield—Franz Beckenbauer, West Germany
Midfield—Eusebio, Portugal
Midfield—Alan Ball, England
Forward—George Best, Northern Ireland
Forward—Stanley Matthews, England
Forward—Alfredo DiStefano, Argentina/Spain
Forward—Ferenc Puskas, Hungary
Substitute—Bobby Moore, England

XIV

On Your Marks

Stan Saplin's 10 Top Headliners in Track and Field History

Once a staff writer for the *New York Journal-American*, Stan Saplin has written track here and abroad, covered several Olympic Games, contributed track articles for magazines and books, and served as a public address announcer for track meets at Madison Square Garden. He was a track commentator for CBS and NBC and has written about track for the *Encyclopedia Britannica*, the *Menke Encyclopedia of Sports*, and other reference works. He considers it a mark of distinction that he saw his No. 1 headliner, the great Paavo Nurmi, *lose* in the Millrose Wannamaker Mile at Madison Square Garden.

1. Paavo Nurmi—In a class by himself. Fifteen outdoor world records from 1,500 meters to 20,000 meters and 9 Olympic gold medals.
2. Roger Bannister—For breaking through the four-minute barrier with his 3:59.4 mile at Oxford in 1954.
3. Bob Beamon—His incredible long-jump of 29 feet 2½

Roger Bannister: First under 4 minutes in the mile.   *UPI*

inches at the Mexico City Olympic Games in 1968 may never be equaled.

4. Cornelius Warmerdam—He pole-vaulted 15 feet or higher 43 times. Not until four years after he retired did anyone else reach 15 feet. Not until 15 years after he retired did anyone surpass his best height of 15 feet 8½ inches.

5. Jesse Owens—He broke three world records and equaled another in a college meet in Ann Arbor in 1935. A year later, he won four gold medals at the Berlin Olympics.

6. Stella Walsh—For winning 41 American championships from 1930 through 1954 in the sprints, field events, and the pentathlon, and for winning the Olympic 100 in 1932 for her native Poland under her original name, Stanislawa Walasiewicz.

7. Al Oerter—For his four consecutive Olympic victories in the discus.

8. Emil Zatopek—For his amazing Olympic triple at Helsinki in 1952—5,000 meters, 10,000 meters, and the marathon.

9. Abebe Bikila—The Ethiopian ran in bare feet to win the Olympic marathon in Rome in 1960. He put on shoes in Tokyo in 1964 and won again, in world-record time, the only repeat marathon winner in Olympic history.

10. Glenn Cunningham—The best, and most exciting, indoor runner of all time.

Bert Nelson's 170 Greatest Track and Field Olympians of All Time

A long-time Olympian-watcher, Bert Nelson is editor and publisher of *Track and Field News,* the bible of the sport.

The incomparable Paavo Nurmi: 9 Olympic gold medals.   *UPI*

MEN

100 Meters
1. Bob Hayes, U.S., 1964
2. Jesse Owens, U.S., 1936
3. Valeri Borzov, USSR, 1972
4. Jim Hines, U.S., 1968
5. Bobby Morrow, U.S., 1956

200 Meters
1. Tommie Smith, U.S., 1968
2. Henry Carr, U.S., 1964
3. Valeri Borzov, USSR, 1972
4. Archie Hahn, U.S., 1904
5. Andy Stanfield, U.S., 1952-56

400 Meters
1. Lee Evans, U.S., 1968
2. Alberto Juantorena, Cuba, 1976
3. Bill Carr, U.S., 1932
4. Otis Davis, U.S., 1960
5. Larry James, U.S., 1968

800 Meters
1. Peter Snell, New Zealand, 1960-64
2. Ted Meredith, U.S., 1912
3. Alberto Juantorena, Cuba, 1976
4. Mel Sheppard, U.S., 1908
5. Tom Hampson, England, 1932

1500 Meters
1. Herb Elliott, Australia, 1960
2. Kip Keino, Kenya, 1968
3. Jack Lovelock, New Zealand, 1936
4. Paavo Nurmi, Finland, 1924
5. Arnold Jackson, Great Britain, 1912

3000 Steeplechase

1. Horace Ashenfelter, U.S., 1952
2. Anders Garderud, Sweden, 1976
3. Volmari Iso-Hollo, Finland, 1932-36
4. Kip Keino, Kenya, 1972
5. Gaston Roelants, Belgium, 1964

5000 Meters

1. Lasse Viren, Finland, 1972-76
2. Emil Zatopek, Czechoslovakia, 1952
3. Paavo Nurmi, Finland, 1924
4. Hannes Kolehmainen, Finland, 1912
5. Murray Halberg, New Zealand, 1960

10,000 Meters

1. Lasse Viren, Finland, 1972-76
2. Vladimir Kuts, USSR, 1956
3. Ville Ritola, Finland, 1924-28
4. Emil Zatopek, Czechoslovakia, 1948-52
5. Paavo Nurmi, Finland, 1920-28

Marathon

1. Abebe Bikila, Ethiopia, 1960-64
2. Emil Zatopek, Czechoslovakia, 1952
3. Frank Shorter, U.S.,1972-76
4. Johnny Hayes, U.S., 1908
5. Hannes Kolehmainen, Finland, 1920

110 Hurdles

1. Lee Calhoun, U.S., 1956-60
2. Earl Thomson, Canada, 1920
3. Rod Milburn, U.S., 1972
4. Forrest Towns, U.S., 1936
5. Syd Atkinson, South Africa, 1924-28

Emil Zatopek achieved an outstanding triple in the 1952 Olympic Games: gold medals in the 5,000- and 10,000-meter competition, and the marathon.   *UPI*

400 Hurdles

1. Edwin Moses, U.S., 1976
2. Glenn Davis, U.S., 1956–60
3. John Aki-Bua, Uganda, 1972
4. F. Morgan Taylor, U.S., 1924–28–32
5. Dave Hemery, Great Britain, 1968

High Jump

1. Charley Dumas, U.S., 1956
2. Dick Fosbury, U.S., 1968
3. Valeri Brumel, USSR, 1960–64
4. Cornelius Johnson, U.S., 1932–36
5. Harold Osborn, U.S., 1924

Pole Vault

1. Frank Foss, U.S., 1920
2. Bob Richards, U.S., 1948–52–56
3. Bob Seagren, U.S., 1968–72
4. Sabin Carr, U.S., 1928
5. Guinn Smith, U.S., 1948

Long Jump

1. Bob Beamon, U.S., 1968
2. Jesse Owens, U.S., 1936
3. Ralph Boston, U.S., 1960–64–68
4. Albert Gutterson, U.S., 1912
5. Ed Hamm, U.S., 1928

Triple Jump

1. Viktor Saneyev, USSR, 1968–72–76
2. Adhemar da Silva, Brazil, 1952–56
3. Naoto Tajima, Japan, 1936
4. Chuhei Nambu, Japan, 1932
5. Josef Schmidt, Hungary, 1960–64

Shot Put

1. Ralph Rose, U.S., 1904–08–12
2. Parry O'Brien, U.S., 1952–56–60–64

Bob Mathias twice won the Olympic decathlon. *UPI*

3. John Kuck, U.S., 1928
4. Randy Matson, U.S., 1964-68
5. Pat McDonald, U.S., 1912

Discus Throw

1. Al Oerter, U.S., 1956-60-64-68
2. Bud Houser, U.S., 1924-28
3. Adolfo Consolini, Italy, 1948-52-56
4. Armas Taipale, Finland, 1912-20
5. Mac Wilkins, U.S., 1976

Hammer Throw

1. Matt McGrath, U.S., 1908-12-20-24
2. John Flanagan, U.S., 1900-04-08
3. Gyula Zsivotzky, Hungary, 1960-64-68-72
4. Josef Csermak, Hungary, 1952
5. Romauld Klim, USSR, 1964-68

Javelin Throw

1. Erlik Lemming, Sweden, 1908-12
2. Egil Danielsen, Denmark, 1956
3. Matti Jarvinen, Finland, 1932
4. Miklos Nemeth, Hungary, 1976
5. Janis Lusis, USSR, 1964-68-72

Decathlon

1. Bob Mathias, U.S., 1948-52
2. Nikolay Avilov, USSR, 1968-72-76
3. Rafer Johnson, U.S., 1956-60
4. Jim Thorpe, U.S., 1912
5. Glenn Morris, U.S., 1936

All-Time Olympians

1. Paavo Nurmi, Finland
2. Al Oerter, U.S.
3. Emil Zatopek, Czechoslovakia
4. Lasse Viren, Finland
5. Bob Mathias, U.S.

WOMEN

100 Meters

1. Wyomia Tyus, U.S., 1964-68
2. Stella Walsh, U.S., 1932-36
3. Renate Stecher, East Germany, 1972-76
4. Wilma Rudolph, U.S., 1960
5. Helen Stephens, U.S., 1936

200 Meters

1. Irena Szewinska, Poland, 1976
2. Renate Stecher, East Germany, 1972
3. Betty Cuthbert, Australia, 1956
4. Edith McGuire, U.S., 1964
5. Raelene Boyle, Australia, 1968-72

400 Meters

1. Irena Szewinska, Poland, 1976
2. Betty Cuthbert, Australia, 1964
3. Monika Zehrt, East Germany, 1972
4. Ann Packer, Great Britain, 1964
5. Colette Besson, France, 1968

800 Meters

1. Tatiana Kazankina, USSR, 1976
2. Madeline Manning, U.S., 1968
3. Ann Packer, Great Britain, 1964
4. Ljudmila Shevcova, USSR, 1960
5. Hildegard Falck, West Germany, 1972

1500 Meters

1. Ludmilla Bragina, USSR, 1972
2. Tatiana Kazankina, USSR, 1976
3. Gunhild Hoffmeister, East Germany, 1972-76
4. Ulrike Klapezynski, East Germany, 1976
5. Paola Cacchi, Italy, 1972

80–100 Meter Hurdles

1. Shirley Strickland de la Hunty, Australia, 1948-52-56
2. Karin Balzer, East Germany, 1964-68
3. Babe Didrikson, U.S., 1932
4. Annelie Erhardt, East Germany, 1972
5. Fanny Blankers-Koen, Holland, 1948

High Jump

1. Iolanda Balas, Rumania, 1956-60-64
2. Mildred McDaniel, U.S., 1956
3. Ulrike Meyfarth, West Germany, 1972
4. Jean Shiley, U.S., 1928-32
5. Rosemarie Ackermann, East Germany, 1976

Long Jump

1. Mary Rand, Great Britain, 1964
2. Elzbieta Krzesinska, Poland, 1956-60
3. Viorica Viscopoleanu, Rumania, 1968
4. Yvette Williams, New Zealand, 1952
5. Vyera Krepkina, USSR, 1960

Shot Put

1. Nadyezhda Chizhova, USSR, 1968-72-76
2. Margitta Gummel, East Germany, 1968-72
3. Galina Zybina, USSR, 1952-56
4. Tamara Press, USSR, 1960-64
5. Ivanka Khristova, Bulgaria, 1972-76

Discus Throw

1. Nina Ponomareva, USSR, 1952-56-60
2. Lia Manoliu, Rumania, 1952-60-64-68
3. Tamara Press, USSR, 1960-64
4. Halina Konopacka, Poland, 1928
5. Olga Fikotova, Czechoslovakia, 1956

Javelin Throw

1. Ruth Fuchs, East Germany, 1972-76

2. Dana Zatopekova, Czechoslovakia, 1952–56–60
3. Inessa Janzeme, USSR, 1956
4. Mihaela Penes, Rumania, 1964–68
5. Elvira Ozolina, USSR, 1960

Pentathlon

1. Irina Press, USSR, 1964
2. Mary Peters, Great Britain, 1972
3. Heide Rosenthal, West Germany, 1972
4. Ingrid Becker, West Germany, 1968
5. Sigrun Siegl, East Germany, 1976

All-Time Olympians

1. Irena Szewinska, Poland
2. Babe Didrikson, U.S.
3. Betty Cuthbert, Australia
4. Fanny Blankers-Koen, Holland
5. Iolanda Balas, Rumania

COURAGEOUS
KINGS POINT, NY

XV

Captains Courageous

Ted Turner's 10 Greatest Skippers

Mr. Turner, principal owner of the Atlanta Braves, reached the pinnacle of his sailing career when he skippered the yacht *Courageous* to victory in the America's Cup in 1977.

1. Christopher Columbus
2. Ferdinand Magellan
3. Francis Drake
4. Captain James Cook
5. Vasco de Gama
6. Henry of Portugal (Sir, the navigator)
7. Horatio Nelson
8. Bud Melges
9. Paul Elvstrom
10.

Ted Turner *(on the stern)* captains the 12-meter yacht "Courageous" on the way to a successful defense of the America's Cup. *UPI*

Walter Slezak's 7 Rules for Boat Guests

Mr. Slezak, a distinguished actor and avid boatman, knows whereof he speaks with regard to safety in boating. He starred with Tallulah Bankhead in the classic movie, "Lifeboat."

1. No hob-nailed shoes aboard.
2. No getting drunk and boisterous.
3. Don't behave as you do in your own home.
4. Don't insist on the radio playing.
5. Don't bring musical instruments on board; anybody doing so will be thrown overboard—with the instruments.
6. Bring your own towels and swimsuits and don't throw wet things on dry clothes of other guests.
7. Don't come aboard in the first place.

Bill Pearsall's 10 Greatest Boating Feats

Bill Pearsall is the author of three books on boating, the producer-writer of numerous motion pictures on boating and water sports, and a member of the editorial advisory board of the magazine *Outdoor-Mariah*. He is a vice-president of the international public relations firm Manning, Selvage & Lee.

1. Sir Francis Chichester—The solo nine-month around-the-world voyage of 65-year-old Sir Francis in his 55-foot *Gypsy Moth IV,* 1966–67, covered 29,630 miles and set numerous records, among them the fastest time for a voyage of its kind and the longest passage

Walter Slezak is at home on his fishing runabout.
New York World-Telegram & Sun

(1,500 miles) by a small sailing vessel without a port of call.

2. Joshua Slocum—The first solo voyage around the world, by Nova Scotia-born Slocum in his 37-foot *Spray*. He started in Boston on April 24, 1895, and finished in Newport, R.I., on June 27, 1898. Distance: 46,000 miles.

3. Ann Davison—The first solo trans-Atlantic crossing by a woman, British-born Davison in her 23-foot sloop *Felicity Ann*. Departed Plymouth, England, May 18, 1952, on a 17-month voyage to the Bahamas via France, Spain, Africa, the Canary Islands, and the West Indies.

4. Robin Lee Graham—The around-the-world voyage of 16-year-old Graham, the youngest ever to make such a voyage. Sailed from San Pedro, Cal., on July 27, 1965, alone except for two kittens, in the 24-foot sloop *Dove*, completing his 33,000-mile trip on April 30, 1970, at Los Angeles.

5. William Robinson—The three-year world cruise, starting in 1928, of 25-year-old Robinson, who, ashore from his ketch *Svaap*, once dined with cannibals and was held captive by an Arab sheik.

6. Tristan Jones—The 13-month voyage above the Arctic, trapped in ice in his 36-foot ketch, *Cresswell*, in May, 1960, accompanied only by Nelson, a three-legged dog.

7. Tristan Jones—A voyage across South America by the Welsh explorer who, in 1973, portaged his 23-foot *Sea Dart* over the Andes in Peru for a downhill river run of 2,700 miles to Buenos Aires.

8. Dougal Robertson—The epic 1,000-mile passage of

Young Robin Lee Graham circumnavigated the world with only a couple of kittens for company.   *UPI*

the Scottish-born Robertson and his crew of five in a nine-foot dinghy, without charts, compass, or instruments, after their 43-foot schooner *Lucette* sank within 60 seconds following an attack by killer whales in the Pacific, June 15, 1972. Robertson and crew survived 37 days in the open ocean and were only 290 miles from Costa Rica, their intended landfall, when rescued by a Japanese fishing vessel.

9. Hal and Margaret Roth—Voyages in a series of small craft taking them through the south and western Pacific, Japan, and the Aleutians, for which they received the Blue Water Medal of the Cruising Club of America in 1971.

10. Samuel Eliot Morrison—Combined voyages of Morrison (1877–1976) who, in the course of his lifetime, followed in the wake of a host of explorers, among them Columbus, Magellan, and Drake.

XVI

Tenpins

Ed Marcou's 10 Greatest Male and 10 Greatest Female Bowlers

Ed Marcou, manager of the National Bowling Hall of Fame, was for many years editor of the *Bowling Journal,* published by the American Bowling Congress.

MALE
(Listed alphabetically)

1. Earl Anthony
2. Don Carter
3. Ned Day
4. Junie McMahon
5. Hank Marino
6. Steve Nagy
7. Joe Norris
8. Jimmy Smith
9. Dick Weber
10. Joe Wilman

FEMALE
(Listed alphabetically)

1. Doris Coburn
2. Shirley Garms
3. Marion Ladewig
4. Floretta McCutcheon
5. Mildred Martorella
6. Dorothy Miller
7. Betty Morris
8. Judy Soutar
9. Marie Warmbier
10. Sylvia Wene

Marcou adds: "I wish I had time to compile my all-time roster of great 'name' bowlers, like Charley Spare, Ned Strike, Jim Pins, etc. But none of these real persons are well known to readers—perhaps it would seem to be mere fiction."

Pat McDonough's 10 Most Remarkable Feats in Bowling History

Pat McDonough covered sports, with an emphasis on bowling, for the *New York World Telegram & Sun* from 1929 until its demise in 1966. He has published his own bowling paper, the *Sports Reporter,* since 1967, and has authored dozens of books and magazine articles on bowling.

1. Elvin Mesger of Sullivan, Mo., rolling a record 27 sanctioned perfect games
2. Allie Brandt of Lockport, N.Y., hitting 297, 289, 300, for a record 886 series in 1939

Marion Ladewig led the women bowlers and became an outstanding instructor.   *Brunswick*

3. Pat Costello setting a women's record with 298, 266, 299, for 863 in 1978

4. Lou Campi beating 14 straight ten-pin greats in TV series, 1958

5. Betty Morris rolling two perfect games in one four-game block, 1977

6. Don Carter winning World Invitational five times in six years, 1957–62

7. Andy Varipapa winning All-Star at age 55 and repeating the following year

8. Earl Anthony accumulating more than $600,000 in career earnings

9. Dick Weber winning titles from 1952 through 1977

10. Floretta McCutcheon beating Jimmy Smith when the latter was acknowledged as the greatest bowler

10 Bowling Oddities

1. Most Consecutive Gutter Balls—19, by Richard Caplette, Danielson, Conn., Sept. 7, 1971

2. Marathon (most games)—1,976, by Bob Atheney, Jr., St. Petersburg, Fla., 265 hours, November 9–11, 1975 (EDITOR'S NOTE: Marathons are not formally recognized by the American Bowling Congress.)

3. Consecutive spares—30, by Howard P. Glover, San Francisco, Calif., August, 1944; by Charles Claybaugh, Anderson, Ind., January 11, 1952; by Ray Wachholz, Oshkosh, Wis., January 17, 1974

4. Consecutive strikes—33, by John Pezzin, Toledo, Ohio, March 4, 1976

5. Consecutive victories—84, by Frank Leonoros, Moose League, Charleston, W.Va., 1948–49

Don Carter was one of bowling's earliest and biggest money-winners. *AMF*

6. 300 Games by One-Armed Men—Frank Parker, Staten Island, N.Y., May 19, 1939: Carl Long, Reading, Pa., November 2, 1961; Joseph C. Schnipke, Sandusky, Ohio, September 11, 1970

7. Youngest Bowler to Record 300 Game—Matt Throne, Millbrae, Calif., August 19, 1971; age: 12 years, 7 months

8. Oldest Bowler to Record 300 Game—Wing Wong, Schenectady, N.Y., May 3, 1972; Henry Kuiper, Three Rivers, Mich., January 9, 1974; Milo Brooks, Kansas City, Mo., December 11, 1977; all at age 74

9. Lineup, Most Years Without Change—25, Crystal Bar, Elkhart (Ind.) Major, started in 1934

10. Most 300 Games By Brothers—13, by Bob (6) and Wayne (7) Pinkalla, Milwaukee, Wis.

SOURCE: *American Bowling Congress Yearbook.*

XVII

"You Don't Say"

Edwin C. Newman's 10 Award-Winning Sports Cliches and Battered Grammar

Critic, correspondent, commentator, and author, Edwin C. Newman has been fascinated by use of the language since his college days at Wisconsin. Known as the house grammarian at NBC, where he has held forth for more than a quarter of a century, Newman has written the best-selling *Strictly Speaking* and *A Civil Tongue*.

1. The player who "suddenly erupted at the plate." The pieces were found scattered along the third base line.
2. Athletes' addiction to "y'know," as with the professional basketball player who spoke of the impossibility of saying when he might be injured, and explained, "Y'know. How do you know? Y'know?"
3. Athletic officials who want to sound important, such as the coach who refused to discuss a disciplinary matter: "This is an internal matter, and we don't care to externalize it."
4. The addiction of those in sports to the suffix, "wise,"

as in "The United States is in good shape, Davis Cup-wise," and "Well, Don's speed was good tonight, but stuffwise, he wasn't all that great."

5. Sports broadcasters whose grip on the language is shaky and who tell of a player who is "loaded with in-experience," or who don't know the difference between "he" and "him," and tell you, "There is nobody be-teen he and the goal line."

6. Pompous sports broadcasters who won't say that two games were called off because of rain but say instead that the games were "victimized by the weather."

7. Athletes who "throw good," "hit good," "block good," have "good hands," have "good running speed," and have "good velocity." Also those who "mean good," "run the curve good," and "come from behind good."

8. Any use of "super" and any use of "capability."

9. Any use of "That has to be," as in "That has to be the best game Oakland ever played." *Why* does it have to be?

10. "This is a hungry team."

Yogi Berra's 10 Best Yogi-isms

1. "I want to thank all those who made this night necessary."—When he was honored at "Yogi Berra Night" in Sportsman's Park, St. Louis.

2. "If you can't imitate him, don't copy him."—To a young player who was trying to emulate the batting style of a veteran player.

3. "Nobody goes there anymore; it's too crowded." —About a popular Minneapolis restaurant.

4. "It's not over until it's over."—Talking about a pennant race.

5. "It gets late early out there."—Explaining why left field is a difficult position to play in Yankee Stadium when shadows fall during a day game in October.

6. "If people don't want to come to the ballpark, how are you gonna stop them?"—Explaining the declining attendance in Kansas City.

7. "We made too many wrong mistakes."—His reason for the Yankees losing the 1960 World Series to the Pittsburgh Pirates.

8. "You observe a lot by watching."—Explaining why he expected to be a successful rookie manager with the Yankees in 1964 despite having no managerial experience.

9. "I usually take a two-hour nap, from one o'clock to four."—When asked what he does the afternoon of a night game.

10. "Anybody who can't tell the difference between a ball hitting wood and a ball hitting concrete must be blind."—In an argument with an umpire, who ruled that a ball hit the concrete wall and was in play; Berra said it hit a wooden barricade beyond the fence and should be a home run.

SOURCE: *The Wit and Wisdom of Yogi Berra,* by Phil Pepe (Hawthorn).

A winning team: Yogi Berra (as N.Y. Mets manager) and his former boss, Casey Stengel, at Kennedy Airport.

UPI

Bill Conlin's 8 Favorite Danny Ozarkisms

Bill Conlin covers the Philadelphia Phillies for the *Philadelphia News* and has been recording the pronouncements of Danny Ozark since the latter became manager of the Phillies in 1973.

1. When asked if there might be a morale problem on the Phillies. "This team's morality is no factor."
2. When his job seemed in jeopardy and general manager Paul Owens was making many trips with the team, Ozark said Owens' presence "was not intimidating and, furthermore, I will not be cohorsed."
3. His evaluation of infielder Mike Andrews: "His limitations are limitless."
4. After being swept by the lowly Atlanta Braves in a three-game series in May, 1976. The sweep, Ozark said, "is beyond my apprehension."
5. After the Phillies had opened a 15½-game lead, only to see it dwindle to 3½ games following a 10-game losing streak, Ozark philosophically reminded the press, "Even Napoleon had his Watergate."
6. After he had outfinessed a rival manager, he humbly accepted the plaudits of the press thusly: "Who knows what evil lurks in the hearts of men except The Shadow."
7. Asked by Ralph Bernstein of the Associated Press why he never gives a straight answer, Ozark replied: "Don't you know I'm a fascist? You know, a guy who says one thing and means another."
8. Asked if he had problems with his players: "Contrary to popular belief, I have always had a wonderful repertoire with my players."

10 Observations of Al McGuire

Former basketball player (St. John's, New York Knicks) and basketball coach (Belmont Abbey, Marquette), Al McGuire has taken a microphone and joined the sports staff of NBC. His witticisms and observations are legend.

1. "I think everyone should go to college and get a degree and then spend six months as a bartender and six months as a cab driver. Then they would really be educated."

2. "Every coach coaches the way he played. I couldn't shoot, so I coached defense."

3. "A team should be an extension of the coach's personality. My teams were arrogant and obnoxious."

4. "Winning is important only in war and surgery."

5. "They call me eccentric. They used to call me nuts. I haven't changed."

6. Noting an overflow crowd in a packed arena: "It looks like a Bronx tenement, all but the wash hanging out."

7. On the huge feet of UCLA's Kiki Vandeweghe: "He must wear drydocks for shoes."

8. On the speed of Dean Meminger: "He's as quick as the last mass at a summer resort."

9. "Only God can be a good official. He's the only guy who can please the other 50 percent."

10. "I was a dance hall player, push and shove. My brother Dick was God-given, a Michelangelo. If I was a horse, I'd be in the second race. Dick would be in the seventh or eighth race."

Lou Holtz's
10 Favorite One-Liners

Known for his wry wit and down-home philosophy, Lou Holtz left North Carolina State and a successful college

coaching career to try his brand of humor with the New York Jets in the NFL in 1976. He finished with a 3-11 record and didn't think it was very funny. The following year he returned to Arkansas and the college coaching ranks.

1. "It's amazing how much you can accomplish when no one cares who gets the credit."
2. "If you can't improve upon silence, be quiet."
3. "It is better to remain quiet and let people think you are a fool than to open your mouth and leave no doubt."
4. "The only exercise some people get is jumping to conclusions."
5. "If you are patting yourself on the back about what you did yesterday, you must not have done much today."
6. "One way to save face is to keep the lower part of it shut."
7. "The only place you can start at the top is digging a hole."
8. "God does not grade on a curve; do right at all times."
9. "You never get ahead of anyone as long as you are trying to get even with him."
10. "I believe education is number one. There have been great players who have been deaf, but never a great one who has been dumb."

10 Things Dick Motta Did Not Say at the White House

Invited to the White House by President Carter after his Washington Bullets won the NBA championship in 1978, coach Dick Motta held his tongue, no small accomplishment. His mouth has preceded him wherever he's gone—Grace Junior High (Idaho), Grace High School, Weber Junior College, Weber State, Chicago Bulls, and Washington Bullets. He is known as one who speaks his mind. But at the White House he did not say these things.

1. "I've coached in better leagues than the NBA."
2. "I don't ask my players if they like me. This is not a popularity contest."
3. "My team comes before my family and my family knows that. And they understand."
4. "You don't have to win everything to be successful, but you have to win everything to be satisfied."
5. "Some of the players' agents are nothing more than flesh peddlers."
6. "This is the black man's sport, the black man's league, the black man's game."
7. "What would I give for Bill Walton? Oh, my team, my wife . . ."
8. "I've never had a job in my life in which failure wasn't predicted for me."
9. "I'm just a converted biology teacher working with some great basketball players, a grown man making money at a game."
10. "I've never been subtle. My frankness has gotten me into all kinds of trouble, but it's the only way I know how to be."

SOURCE: *Stuff It: The Story of Dick Motta.* by Dick Motta and Jerry Jenkins (Chilton).

15 Famous Sports Quotations

1. "Hit 'em where they ain't."—Wee Willie Keeler, explaining the batting technique that allowed him to

make 2,932 hits in 19 big league seasons although he was only 5-4½.

2. "Is Brooklyn still in the league?"—New York Giants manager Bill Terry about the hated Brooklyn Dodgers. The sixth-place Dodgers responded by beating the Giants late in the season, knocking them out of first place and enabling the St. Louis Cardinals to win the National League pennant.

3. "The bigger they come, the harder they fall."—Challenger Bob Fitzsimmons, 167 pounds, commenting on his opponent, champion James J. Jeffries, 206 pounds, prior to their rematch for the heavyweight title in San Francisco on July 25, 1902. Jeffries KOd Fitzsimmons in the 8th round to retain his title.

4. "The Giants is dead."—Brooklyn Dodgers manager Charlie Dressen in August, 1953. The New York Giants were floundering and the Dodgers were on their way to a second straight pennant. Dressen assured reporters that the Giants wouldn't repeat their 1951 miracle. They didn't.

5. "Win one for the Gipper."—Notre Dame football coach Knute Rockne, in one of his stirring halftime speeches, imploring his players to go out and win a game in honor of former Notre Dame halfback George Gipp, who lay near death in a hospital.

6. "I never called one wrong."—Famous baseball umpire, Bill Klem, summing up his career.

7. "We wuz robbed."—Manager Joe Jacobs after Jack Sharkey had been awarded a questionable 15-round decision, enabling him to regain the heavyweight championship of the world from Jacobs' fighter, Max Schmeling.

8. "Good field, no hit."—Cuban scout Mike Gonzalez in a telegram scouting report on a young player, Moe

Umpire Bill ("I never called one wrong") Klem. *UPI*

Berg, upon request for same by the Brooklyn Dodgers in 1924.

9. "Winning isn't everything, it's the only thing."—Vince Lombardi, coach of the Green Bay Packers of the NFL.

10. "I'd rather be lucky than good."—Lefty Gomez, pitcher for the New York Yankees, after winning a game in which every ball hit went into a fielder's glove.

11. "He can run, but he can't hide."—Heavyweight champion Joe Louis, commenting on his challenger Billy Conn, who was extremely fast on his feet and noted for his ability to dance away from his opponent. On June 18, 1941, in New York's Polo Grounds, Conn ran for 12 rounds, then was knocked out in the 13th.

12. "Nice guys finish last."—The appraisal by manager Leo Durocher, commenting on the need to be mean to win.

13. "Wait 'til next year."—The perennial cry of fans of the Brooklyn Dodgers, who repeatedly finished second-best to the New York Yankees in the World Series.

14. "Luck is the residue of design."—The philosophy of Branch Rickey, who built championship baseball teams in Brooklyn, St. Louis, and Pittsburgh.

15. "The game isn't over until the last man is out."—Anonymous.

Vince Lombardi's Super Bowl feats weren't everything; they were the only thing. *Ken Regan*

XVIII

A Cavalcade
of Sports Figures

Stan Isaacs' Numbers
Hall of Fame

Stan Isaacs, currently television sports columnist of *News-day*, is a list-maker, too. His annual rating of the best chocolate ice cream in the United States is awaited eagerly by anyone who ever licked a cone.

On March 6, 1971, Isaacs presented his "Numbers Hall of Fame," which he described as follows:

"This is a roll call of distinction among athletes in all sports by the numbers they wore on their backs. . . . This is a subjective listing leaning heavily on the archivist's prejudices, meaning there was no way Mel Ott could be kept off it; and there is some leaning toward New York athletes.

"Note I: Numbers didn't come into existence in baseball until the late 1920s, so people like Ty Cobb and Christy Mathewson could not qualify.

"Note II: This is one Hall of Fame where Satchel Paige will not go in the back of the room. Without him no Hall is complete, and his presence honors us.

"We welcome them all, with apologies to the Lou (No. 4) Gehrigs, Bobby (No. 4) Orrs, Mel (No. 7) Heins, and Whizzer (No. 24) Whites, who were edged out. Here they are:"

0 Johnny O. Olszewski, pro football . . . was no cipher as a ball-carrier.

00 Jim Otto, Oakland football . . . that goes double for him as a center. Johnny (Double No-Hit) Vander Meer refused to wear the number.

1/8 Eddie Gaedel . . . Bill Veeck's wonderful midget.

1 Gump Worsley . . . No. 1 is a hockey goalie's number, and Worsley wore it with *joie de vivre* as a Ranger.

1A Coaltown . . . the other half of the famous entry with Citation.

2 Leo Durocher . . . he's been wearing it since the 1930s.

3 Babe Ruth . . . the all-time champ.

4 Mel Ott . . . if you grew up as a Giants fan in the 1930s and '40s, there can be none other.

5 Joe DiMaggio . . . "We want you on our side"—and Mrs. Robinson, too.

6 Bill Russell . . . with regrets to Stan Musial and Al Kaline.

7 Hank Luisetti . . . the Stanford man whose one-hand shot revolutionized basketball.

8 Carl Yastrzemski . . . he wouldn't have made it as a potato farmer.

9 Gordie Howe . . . over Maurice "the Rocket" Richard and Bobby Hull, yet.

10 Pelé . . . the soccer immortal from Brazil, and the number tells you his position is inside left.

11 Carl Hubbell . . . Mel Ott's roommate; the man with the golden crooked arm.

12 Joe Namath . . . for his arm and his mouth.

13 Ralph Branca . . . who else?

14 Bob Cousy . . . for his playing and his "r" speech defect.

15 Dick McGuire . . . to go with Cousy in the backcourt.

16 Whitey Ford . . . an old smoothie.

17 John Havlicek . . . for personifying hustle.

18 Mel Harder, Cleveland Indians . . . a quiet measure of dignity here.

19 Bob Feller . . . "Rapid Robert" was a grand nickname.

20 Frank Robinson . . . Most Valuable Player in both leagues; the only one.

21 Roberto Clemente . . . he hit Warren (No. 21) Spahn like he owned him.

22 Elgin Baylor . . . with regrets to Dave DeBusschere and Bob Hayes.

23 Bobby Thomson . . . see No. 13.

24 Willie Mays . . . "see No. 24 catch that ball hit by Vic Wertz."

25 Gus Johnson . . . the rebounding, astounding Baltimore Bullet.

26 Maurice Stokes, St. Francis of Loretto . . . to have seen him play once was never to forget him.

27 Pete Reiser . . . Charley Dressen appropriated No. 7 from him when Dressen joined the Dodgers.

28 Preacher Roe, Brooklyn Dodgers . . . he admitted he threw the spitball.

29 Satchel Paige . . . he wore this number as a rookie with the Cleveland Indians in 1948, when he had a 6-1 record.

30 Tuffy Brashun . . . the first queen of the roller derby.

31 Jack Twyman . . . he always knew where the basket was.

32 Jim Brown . . . with a boo-hoo to Sandy Koufax.

33 Sammy Baugh . . . the greatest quarterback of them all.

34 Cookie Gilchrist, Buffalo Bills . . . on ability—and charm.

35 Sal Maglie . . . by a close shave over Doc Blanchard.

36 Robin Roberts . . . old blood, sweat, and tears.

37 Casey Stengel . . . "We could hardly wait to get to you, doctor."

38 Roger Craig, Mets . . . he once changed his number to try to break a losing streak.

39 Roy Campanella . . . he loved the game.

40 Gale Sayers . . . and his wife says he can't dance.

41 Glenn Davis . . . "Come on inside, Mr. Outside."

42 Jackie Robinson . . . and isn't it amazing how humble he was that first year?

43 Carl "Spider" Lockhart . . . the Giants' demon tackler and sweet guy.

44 Henry Aaron . . . by the width of a Wheaties flake over Jerry West.

45 Emlen Tunnell . . . another smoothie.

46 Brooks Lawrence, Cincinnati Reds . . . he had a certain style.

47 Claude "Monk" Simons . . . Tulane star of the first Sugar Bowl and in the college Hall of Fame.

48 Karl Spooner, Brooklyn Dodgers . . . a sore-arm guy who symbolizes all the bright careers that were nipped in the bud.

49 Tom Landry, football Giants . . . a coach on the field.

50 Goose Tatum, Globetrotters . . . "In the beginning was a clown."

51 Dick Butkus, Chicago Bears . . . for sex appeal.

52 Joe Pignatano, Met coach . . . help, help.

53 Don Drysdale . . . he once threw a soft pitch, a cookie, to ex-roommate Duke Snider.

54 Lucious Jackson, Philadelphia 76ers . . . when he came back from the 1964 Tokyo Olympics wearing a gold medal, teammate Johnny Kerr looked at it,

turned it over, and said: "Ahh, it says, 'Made in Japan.'"

55 E.J. Holub, Kansas City football . . . over Spud (Yankee batting practice pitcher) Murray.

56 Jim Bouton . . . "Stop giggling and come on in, Jim."

57 Johnny Blood . . . the Green Bay swashbuckler who also wore Nos. 14, 15, 20, 24, 55 at various pit stops.

58 Dixie Howell, 1934 Alabama football . . . he passed to Don (No. 14) Hutson.

59 Lonnie Warwick, Minnesota Vikings . . . hooray for linebackers.

60 Chuck Bednarik, at Penn and the Philadelphia Eagles . . . that was a clean shot he hit Frank Gifford.

61 Curly Culp, Kansas City football . . . and a hurrah for interior linemen.

62 Charley Trippi, 1945 Georgia football . . . would you believe that some people called him "the Scintillating Sicilian?"

63 Willie Lanier, Kansas City football . . . another linebacker.

64 Jerry Kramer, Green Bay . . . the pen is mightier than the block.

65 Houston Antwine, Boston Patriots . . . what's in a name, indeed.

66 Bulldog Turner . . . from the days when they were the grizzly Bears.

67 Dave Herman, Jets . . . he means to be mean.

68 Gale Gillingham, Green Bay . . . can you top this?

69 Paul Zimmerman, Columbia Old Blue . . . rugby ruffian.

70 Sam Huff, Giants football . . . rough, tough, took no guff, etc.

71 Alex Karras, Detroit Lions . . . a clown and a prince of players.

72 George Cafego, 1940 Tennessee halfback . . . his nickname: "Bad News."

73 Leo Nomellini, San Francisco 49er lineman . . . on all-time league team.

74 Merlin Olsen, Los Angeles Rams . . . as big as all Utah.

75 Deacon Jones, Los Angeles Rams . . . as good as he thinks he is.

76 Buddy Young, All-America Conference football . . . the most artful dodger of them all.

77 Red Grange, Illinois . . . the most famous sports number.

78 Bubba Smith, Baltimore Colts . . . he comes to kill.

79 Roosevelt Brown, football Giants . . . from 27th round draft choice to fame.

80 Tom Fears . . . combined one day with Elroy (No. 40) Hirsch to catch 550 yards of passes thrown by Norm (No. 11) Van Brocklin.

81 Bill Swiacki, Columbia end . . . "Did you see Bill Swiacki make that catch!"

82 Raymond Berry, Baltimore Colts . . . he worked his football-catching fingers to the bone.

83 George Sauer, Jets . . . for suggesting the honor of a "pre-game ball."

84 Jack Snow, LA Rams pass catcher . . . can you top this?

85 Del Shofner, football Giants . . . Y.A. (No. 14) Tittle's favorite playmate.

86 Brud Holland, 1938 Cornell and . . . a college president turned ambassador.

87 Len Ford, 1947 Michigan and . . . a terrific Cleveland Browns pro.

88 John Mackey, Colts . . . voted the league's all-time top tight end.

89 Gino Marchetti, Colts . . . he has almost assumed a mythical quality.

90 Glenn Dobbs, Brooklyn Dodgers football . . . magnificently led team to an 0–11 record.

91 Johnny Strzykalski, San Francisco 49ers circa 1946 . . . his nickname: "Strike."

92 Joe Vetrano, 49er kicker . . . his nickname: "Joe the Toe."

93 Erich Segal, author . . . Boston marathon, 1967.

94 Dom Principe, Brooklyn Dodgers . . . we're grateful the old AAC used numbers in the 90s.

95 Frankie Grable . . . star of the Satchels S.A.C., softball champs of the Kent Avenue Brooklyn playground, 1941.

96 Bill Voiselle, NY Giants . . . he wore it one night in honor of his home town, Ninety-Six, S.C.

97 Monk Gafford, Miami Seahawks, AAC . . . a tough guy.

98 Tom Harmon . . . the second famous number of our time, and his wife, Elyse Knox, was a sweet number, too.

99 George Mikan . . . basketball's first titan.

Note: Century Milstead, Yale hero circa 1920s, didn't wear No. 100—they didn't wear numbers then.

Bob Paul's 10 Most Significant Olympic Medalists

Bob Paul has been studying for a doctorate of Olympic trivia for the last half-century, while pursuing relentlessly recognition for the underdog, the little-known and the talented woman athlete. Paul is Director of Communications for the United States Olympic Committee.

1. James B. Connolly, 1896, triple jump gold medalist

When Harvard denied him a leave of absence to take part in the Games of the last Olympiad, he kissed Harvard goodbye and won the first gold medal awarded in the modern Olympic Games. Lack of a Harvard diploma didn't prevent him from becoming a well-known author of sea stories.

2. Debbie Meyer, 1968, three gold medals in swimming

Can you believe that her winning time in the 400-meter freestyle (4:31.8) was more than 30 seconds faster than the mark set by Johnny "Tarzan" Weissmuller in 1924 (5:04.2)?

3. Emil Zatopek, Czechoslovakia, 1952

After winning his favorite 5,000 and 10,000-meter races, he tried the marathon, a distance he had never raced before. He posted the fastest winning time to that date for the 26-mile, 385-yard endurance test (2 hours, 23 minutes, 3.2 seconds), and won by 4½ minutes over his nearest competitor.

4. Eddie Eagan

The Yale graduate is the only gold medalist from the Olympic summer *and* winter competitions. As a Yale senior, he won the light heavyweight boxing championship at Antwerp in 1920. Twelve years later, he was a member of the United States' winning four-man bobsled team at Lake Placid.

5. Alvin Kraenzlein, University of Pennsylvania/University of Wisconsin

The only man ever to win four gold medals in individual events on the Olympic track and field program. At Paris in 1900, he prevailed in the long jump, 60 meters, 110-meter hurdles, and 200-meter hurdles.

6. Marjorie Gestring, United States

In 1936 at Berlin, she struck a blow for kids of either sex. At the age of 13 years, 4 months, she won the women's springboard title and recognition as the youngest gold medalist in the modern Olympic Games.

7. Fannie Blankers-Koen, the Netherlands

In 1948, she said it for motherhood, although antiquated

rules restricted her to four events (she was the world record holder in the long jump, but elected not to compete in the event). She captured four gold medals for her husband and family, and was dubbed "Fabulous Fannie."

8. Vera Caslavska, Czechoslovakia, Olympic women's all-around gymnastics champion in 1964 and 1968

Perhaps the foremost contributor to the popularity of the sport to the uninitiated via television. After her '68 triumph, she was married in an Olympic ceremony to a teammate from track and field, Josef Odlozil.

9. George Foreman, United States, Olympic heavyweight boxing champion

Won the Olympic title with only 19 previous fights before the 1968 Olympic Games in Mexico City. "Long may she wave." That is the American flag he unfurled in the ring after receiving his gold medal.

Fabulous Fannie Blankers-Koen won four gold medals in the 1948 Olympic Games.
                                                         UPI

10. Anders Haugen, United States

Victor on a recount. Fifty years after the 1924 inaugural Olympic Games at Chamonix, France, a Norwegian sports statistician uncovered a mathematical error in the computation of the final standings in the Nordic combined ski event (cross-country ski race and ski jumping). The bronze medal was recovered from the Norwegian recipient and bestowed upon Haugen in impressive ceremonies in Oslo in 1974.

Bob Paul adds: "My apologies to my many, many other friends from the United States and other countries who have performed notably and with great success and will be included on my list for the all-time great guys and gals who have climbed the highest step of the Olympic victory podium all over the world."

12 Athlete–Doctors

1. Renee Richards   (tennis player-ophthalmologist)
2. Bobby Brown   (baseball player-cardiologist)

Renee Richards switched from a career in ophthalmology to pro tennis.
UPI

  3. Gary Cuozzo   (pro football player-dentist)
  4. Tenley Albright   (Olympic figure skating champion-surgeon)
  5. Danny Fortmann   (pro football player-surgeon)
  6. Sammy Lee   (Olympic diving champion-ear, nose, and throat specialist)
  7. Ernie Vandeweghe   (pro basketball player-pediatrician)
  8. Delano Meriwether   (sprinter-hematologist)
  9. Ron Taylor   (baseball player-internist)
 10. George "Doc" Medich   (baseball player-surgeon)
 11. George Sheehan   (marathon runner-cardiologist)
 12. Rick Herrscher   (baseball player-orthodontist)

Phyllis Hollander's Dozen and 1 Significant Women Athletes

Phyllis Hollander, senior editor of Associated Features, is author of *American Women in Sports* and *100 Greatest Women in Sports*. She is also co-author (with L. Herkimer) of *The Complete Book of Cheerleading* and co-editor (with Z. Hollander) of *They Dared To Lead* and *It's the Final Score That Counts*.

  1. Babe Didrikson—Won the National AAU outdoor championships in five events (80 meter hurdles, high jump, shot put, javelin, baseball throw) in 1932, played championship basketball, and was winner of two gold medals and one silver medal at the 1932 Olympics; set an all-time record for women's golf in the 1946–47 season by winning 17 tournaments in a row; chosen Woman Athlete of the Half-Century in

1950 Associated Press poll of the nation's sportswriters; after courageous comeback from major cancer surgery, she won seven more golf tournaments before being defeated by the disease in 1956.

2. Gertrude Ederle—At age 17 was holder of 18 world's distance swimming records and was an Olympic gold medalist in the 400-meter relay; was the first American woman to swim across the English Channel from France to England. Until that day in August, 1926, only five men had succeeded in conquering the Channel. Ederle's time was a record 14 hours, 31 minutes.

3. Althea Gibson—Poor black from the streets of Harlem, she was the first of her race to play in the United States National Tennis Championships (1950) and Wimbledon (1951). In 1957 and 1958, she won both these tournaments.

4. Billie Jean King—Libber and lobber, King shared the record of 19 Wimbledon titles with America's Elizabeth Ryan, who won hers in the '20s and '30s as a doubles player. The modern day queen of tennis, Ms. King was the first woman to sign a pro contract with a female tournament group; the first female athlete to win more than $100,000 in prize money ($117,000 in 1971); the first woman to defeat a man in a challenge match (Bobby Riggs in 1973, 6-4, 6-3, 6-3); and the first woman coach of a professional co-ed team (player-coach of the Philadelphia Freedoms). She, Helen Wills Moody, and Molla Mallory share the distinction of being ranked No. 1 in the United States the most times (7).

5. Kathy Kusner—Leading international dressage rider and winner of an Olympic silver medal in 1972, Kathy was the first woman to be granted a jockey license (in 1968) by the Maryland Racing Commission. This was

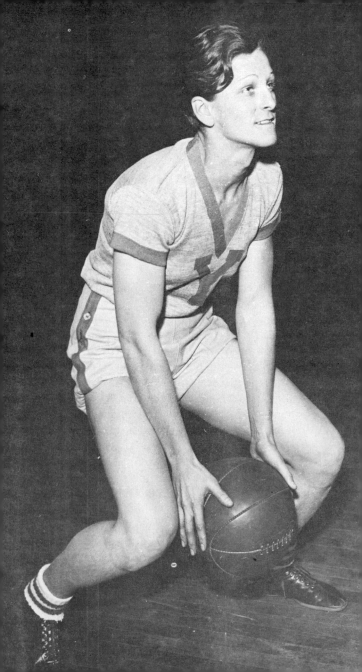

a court victory which opened the doors to women jockeys on thoroughbred tracks everywhere.

6. Andrea Mead Lawrence—In 1948, at age 16, she was the youngest member of a United States Olympic ski team. In 1952, she became the first American skier to win two gold medals.

7. Ann Curtis—In 1944 she became the first woman and the first swimmer to win the Sullivan Award as the outstanding amateur athlete of the year. She was the first woman to swim 100 yards in less than one minute, she set 4 world freestyle records, 18 American records, won 31 national championships, and brought home two gold and one silver medals from the 1948 Olympic Games.

8. Pat McCormick—The only American diver to twice win two gold medals in consecutive Olympics, 1952

(Opposite) Before her Olympic feats, Babe Didrikson was a championship basketball player.   *UPI*

(Below) New York gave Gertrude "Trudy" Ederle a ticker-tape parade after she swam the English Channel in 1926.   *UPI*

and 1956, and the second female winner of the Sullivan Award.

9. Diana Nyad—A doctoral candidate in comparative literature and Barnard College swimming coach, this tenacious and courageous athlete attempts long-distance swims the way others climb mountains. Although failing in her first attempt at the super-human task of swimming from Cuba to Key West, Florida, a distance of 103 miles through open water, her other marathon swims proved her exceptional skill and endurance. In one period of five years (1960–65), she covered 25 miles in the Suez Canal, 67 miles in the North Sea, 22 miles in the Nile, 32 miles off the coast of Mexico, 26 miles in the Parana River, 22 miles across the Bay of Naples, 31 miles from St. Thomas to Virgin Gorda, 32 miles on Lake Ontario, and 50 miles from the Great Barrier Reef to Australia.

10. Wilma Rudolph—A victim of polio as a child, she won three gold medals in the 1960 Olympics and was the first female winner of the UPI Athlete of the Year poll. She was the third female recipient of the Sullivan Award in 1961.

11. Eleonora Sears—A member of Boston high society in the early 1900s, liberated Eleonora shocked the prudish American public by riding astride, racing cars, flying planes, and following such all-male pursuits as hunting, fishing, and canoeing. In tennis, she won the national doubles title four times, mixed doubles once, and was a finalist in singles twice. She was captain of the International Squash Racquets team, president of the Women's Squash Association, and the first national title-holder in 1928. In her forties, Eleonora took up long-distance walking: 47 miles from Providence to Boston, 73 miles from Newport to Boston, 42½ miles from Fountainebleu to the Ritz Bar in Paris.

12. Kathy Switzer—Ran unofficially in the 26-mile Boston Marathon in 1967. The resulting publicity pressured marathon officials into permitting women to compete.

13. Sheila Young—The first athlete to win world championships in both track cycling and speed skating. In 1976 at the Winter Olympics, she became the first American to bring home three medals from the Winter Games—gold in the 500 meters, silver in the 1,500 meters, and bronze in the 1,000 meters.

12 Well-Known, or Infamous, Tobacco Chewers

1. Danny Murtaugh—He delighted in picking out sports writers wearing white shoes and spraying the shoes with juice.

2. Ralph Houk—His thing was to sneak up behind unsuspecting, preoccupied players, and shoot a squirt in their back pockets.

3. Steve Hamilton—One fateful day in Kansas City, while pitching for the Yankees, he swallowed his chaw and threw up all over the pitcher's mound.

4. Catfish Hunter—"I started chewing in high school. My coach wouldn't let us chew bubble gum ever since a guy on first base blew a bubble and missed the steal sign. I chew all the time, even at home, but never when I'm pitching because I'm afraid of swallowing the thing."

5. Tobacco Johnny Lanning—His nickname tells it all.

6. Nellie Fox—"I always thought he had the mumps," says Yogi Berra, a nonchewer.

7. Harvey Kuenn—"I believe he chewed when he slept," says Al Rosen.

8. Sparky Lyle

9. Rocky Bridges

10. Johnny Sain

11. Don Zimmer—"He looks like a gerbil," says Bill Lee.
12. Rod Carew

20 Remarkable Comebacks

1. 1978 Yankees—Trailing the first-place Boston Red
Sox by 14 games on July 19, the Yankees won 52 of
their last 73 games to finish the regular season tied
with Boston. They then beat the Red Sox in a one-
game playoff to win the AL East title, beat the Kansas
City Royals in four games to win the AL pennant, and
beat the Los Angeles Dodgers in six games to win their
second consecutive World Series, thereby climaxing
the greatest comeback in American League history.
2. Muhammad Ali—Convicted for draft evasion, Ali was
stripped of his heavyweight title, then had his license
revoked. Refusing to compromise his principles, Ali

Nellie Fox did not have the mumps.   *Chicago White Sox*

faced a jail sentence and was exiled from the ring for 42 months. He returned on October 26, 1970, in Atlanta, Georgia, stopping Jerry Quarry in the third round. Four years and four days later, he completed his comeback in Kinshasa, Zaire, KOing George Foreman in the eighth round to regain his heavyweight championship.

3. Ben Hogan—An auto accident on a rain-slicked Texas highway left the great golfer near death in 1949. Doctors fought to pull him through, then feared he might never walk again. Playing golf seemed out of the question, but 10 months after his near-fatal accident, Bantam Ben returned to win the United States Open for the second time.

4. Buckpasser—Twice shelved with quarter cracks, out of the Kentucky Derby and the Preakness, the great colt became the first 3-year-old to earn $1 million in purses. After another long absence because of quarter cracks, he returned to racing to become 1966 Horse of the Year.

5. Joe Di-Maggio—After missing half of the 1949 season with a bone spur on his heel, Joe DiMaggio returned for a three-game series in Boston. He hit four home runs and drove in nine runs in leading the New York Yankees to a sweep of the three games and the American League pennant.

6. John Surtees—Near death after a serious accident on the track, the English auto racer vowed he would drive again. The next year, 1964, he won the World Driving Championship.

7. Toronto Maple Leafs—Down three games to none in the 1942 Stanley Cup finals, the Leafs beat the Detroit Red Wings in the next four games to take the Cup, the only time in Stanley Cup history a team had come back from a 3-0 deficit.

In the course of his comeback, Muhammad Ali was defeated by Joe Frazier *(left)* in 1971. *UPI*

8. The Miracle Braves—In last place on July 4, 1914, the
   Boston Braves made up a 15-game deficit to win the
   National League pennant by 10½ games over the New
   York Giants, then beat the Philadelphia A's in four
   straight games in the World Series. It remains the only
   time in history a team has gone from last place on July
   4 to win a pennant, and the only time a team has made
   up as much as a 15-game deficit at any point in the
   season.

9. Lester Patrick—At the age of 45, the coach of the New
   York Rangers, who was not a goaltender during his
   playing days, donned the pads and went into the net
   after his only goalie was injured. With Patrick in goal,

Lester Patrick became a goalie for a night at age 45.   *Hockey Hall of Fame*

the Rangers beat the Montreal Canadiens in a 1928 Stanley Cup game.

10. Ted Williams—After spending two years as a fighter pilot in Korea, Williams returned to the Boston Red Sox only to sustain a broken collar bone. Returning from that injury, he batted .345 in 1954. He planned to retire after that season, but was persuaded to return. He did, leading the league in batting in 1958 at age 40 and finally retiring in 1960, at age 42.

11. Gordie Howe—The leading point scorer in NHL history, he retired in 1971, at age 43, after 25 years. Impelled by the desire to play with his sons, Mark and Marty, Howe returned at age 45 to play for the Houston Aeros of the World Hockey Association and was named the league's Most Valuable Player for the 1973–74 season.

12. Harrison Dillard—Beaten in his specialty, the high hurdles, in the 1948 Olympic Games, Dillard came back in the 100-yard dash to score a tremendous upset and win the gold medal.

13. Y.A. Tittle—Considered washed-up with the San Francisco 49ers, the bald quarterback was traded to the New York Giants and led them to three division championships, the last at age 39.

14. Joe Louis—Knocked out in the 12th round by Max Schmeling in 1936 for his first defeat in 28 professional fights, Louis waited 2 years and 3 days to avenge that defeat, KOing Schmeling in the first round of their fight on June 22, 1938.

15. John Hiller—Felled by a heart attack in 1971, his life in danger, his promising career seemingly at an end, the Detroit Tigers relief pitcher fought his way back in 1973, saving a record 38 games and being named "Fireman of the Year."

16. Princeton-Michigan—Down by 14 points with 4½ minutes to go, the Michigan Wolverines fought back

to beat Princeton in the semi-finals of the ECAC Holiday Festival Basketball Tournament at Madison Square Garden in 1964.

17. Jeff Farrell—Considered America's best bet for a gold medal in the swimming competition of the 1960 Olympics, he was knocked out of action by an emergency appendectomy. He was taken to the Olympics as a substitute, but not expected to compete. When another swimmer became ill, Farrell swam in the 400-meter relay and anchored the United States' team to victory in record time.

18. Yale Crew—Faced with elimination in the 1956 Olympic Games after finishing third in the first heat, Yale came back from the brink of elimination to win the next two heats and take the gold medal in the eight-oared event.

19. Helen Wills Moody—In voluntary retirement for two years, Mrs. Moody returned to the tennis wars and became the first woman to win Wimbledon 7 times.

20. Boston Red Sox—Ninth in American League in 1966, the Red Sox came back to win the pennant in 1967. No team had ever come from so deep in the standings one year to the top the next.

Birth Dates of 62 Great Athletes

1. Henry Aaron—February 5, 1934
2. Kareem Abdul-Jabbar—April 16, 1947
3. Muhammad Ali—January 17, 1942
4. Eddie Arcaro—February 19, 1916
5. Sammy Baugh—March 17, 1914
6. Jim Brown—February 17, 1936
7. Dick Button—July 18, 1929
8. Rod Carew—October 1, 1945
9. Don Carter—July 29, 1926
10. Wilt Chamberlain—August 21, 1936

11. Ty Cobb—December 18, 1886
12. Bob Cousy—August 9, 1928
13. Glenn Cunningham—August 4, 1909
14. Jack Dempsey—June 24, 1895
15. Joe DiMaggio—November 25, 1914
16. Julius Erving—February 22, 1950
17. Bob Feller—November 3, 1918
18. A.J. Foyt—January 16, 1935
19. Pancho Gonzalez—May 9, 1928
20. Otto Graham—December 6, 1921
21. Red Grange—June 13, 1903
22. Ben Hogan—August 13, 1912
23. Gordie Howe—March 31, 1928
24. Reggie Jackson—May 18, 1946
25. Rafer Johnson—August 18, 1934
26. Bobby Jones—March 17, 1902
27. Jean Claude Killy—August 30, 1943
28. Billie Jean King—November 22, 1943
29. Sandy Koufax—December 30, 1935
30. Jack Kramer—August 1, 1921
31. Joe Louis—May 13, 1914
32. Mickey Mantle—October 20, 1931
33. Rocky Marciano—September 1, 1923
34. Willie Mays—May 6, 1931
35. George Mikan—June 18, 1924
36. Joe Namath—May 31, 1943
37. Jack Nicklaus—January 21, 1940
38. Bobby Orr—March 20, 1948
39. Jesse Owens—September 12, 1913
40. Pelé—October 23, 1940
41. Satchel Paige—September 18, 1899;
September 11, 1904;
July 28, 1905;
July 7, 1906;
July 18, 1908;
August 27, 1908;

> September 18, 1908;
> September 22, 1908;
> or July 22, 1909

42. Arnold Palmer—September 10, 1929
43. Maurice Richard—August 4, 1921
44. Oscar Robertson—November 24, 1938
45. Jackie Robinson—January 31, 1919
46. Sugar Ray Robinson—May 3, 1920
47. Pete Rose—April 14, 1941
48. Al Rosen—February 29, 1924
49. Bill Russell—February 12, 1934
50. Babe Ruth—February 6, 1895
51. Tom Seaver—November 17, 1944
52. Secretariat—March 30, 1970
53. Willie Shoemaker—August 19, 1931
54. O.J. Simpson—July 7, 1947
55. Sam Snead—May 27, 1912
56. Mark Spitz—February 10, 1950
57. John L. Sullivan—October 15, 1858
58. Jim Thorpe—May 28, 1888
59. Bill Tilden—February 10, 1893
60. Johnny Unitas—May 7, 1933
61. Johnny Weissmuller—June 2, 1904
62. Cy Young—March 29, 1867

Kyle Rote Jr.'s 10 All-Time Superstars (Based on the ABC Superstars Competition)

Kyle Rote Jr., of the NASL Houston Hurricane, is the only athlete to win the Superstars competition three times, in 1974, 1976, and 1977.

Tennis—Peter Snell, runner
Golf—Dick Anderson, football player
Swimming—Brian Budd, soccer player
Weightlifting—Brian Oldfield, shotputter
Bowling—Paul Blair, baseball player
100-yard dash—O.J. Simpson, football player

Half-mile run—Bob Seagren, pole vaulter
Mile bike ride—Wayne Grimditch, water skier
Obstacle course—Lynn Swann, football player
Baseball hitting—Dan Pastorini, football player

Associated Press' 22 Greatest Women Athletes of the First Half of the Twentieth Century

1. Mildred "Babe" Didrikson Zaharias, golf, track and field.
2. Helen Wills Moody, tennis
3. Stella Walsh, track and field
4. Fannie Blankers-Koen, track and field
5. Gertrude Ederle, swimming
6. Suzanne Lenglen, tennis
7. Alice Marble, tennis
8. Ann Curtis, swimming
9. Sonja Henie, figure skating
10. Helen Stephens, track and field
11. Eleanor Holm, swimming
12. Patty Berg, golf
13. Helene Madison, swimming
14. Glenna Collett Vare, golf
15. Mary K. Browne, golf, tennis
16. Eleonora Sears, hiking, tennis, squash racquets
17. Helen Jacobs, tennis
18. Louise Suggs, golf
19. Joyce Wethered, golf
20. Zoe Ann Olsen, swimming
21. Barbara Ann Scott, figure skating
22. Mildred Burke, wrestling

16 Famous Sports Walkouts

1. Eddie Sawyer—He had led the Philadelphia Phillies to their first National League championship in 36 years, winning with the so-called "Whiz Kids" in 1950. After finishing fifth and fourth the next two years, Sawyer was

replaced. But his successors did no better and Sawyer was summoned back in the middle of the 1958 season. The Phillies finished seventh that year and eighth the next. Fed up with his team's lack of progress and disappointed at the material he had been given, Sawyer could suffer no longer. He went through spring training in 1960 and resigned after the Phillies lost on opening day.

2. Gene Conley-Pumpsie Green—The two Boston Red Sox players were missing when the team left New York after a series there. They had jumped the team. Rumors circulated that, on a whim, they had decided to fly to Israel. Both returned within a week, refusing to reveal where they had been.

3. Bill Winfrey—After training thoroughbreds with unusual success for the Phipps' Wheatley Stable, Winfrey one day decided he had had enough and quit the racing business without an explanation.

4. Sandy Koufax—Plagued by an arthritic condition, Koufax walked away from major league baseball and a lucrative contract while he was the greatest pitcher in the game. When he quit, after the 1966 season, he had led the National League in ERA for the last 5 seasons, in victories for the last 2, and in strikeouts for the last 2. He was only 31 years old at the time, in the prime years for a pitcher. "I don't want to live the rest of my life as a cripple," he explained.

5. Jay Berwanger—As the first winner of the prestigious Heisman Trophy in 1935, Berwanger, an end for the University of Chicago, was in great demand among professional teams. But he resisted all offers and walked away from pro football, choosing to enter private business instead.

6. Rocky Marciano—With no more worlds to conquer after winning all 49 of his fights as a professional—all but six by KO—he retired from the ring on April 27, 1956, only the second heavyweight champion to retire

undefeated. The first was Gene Tunney.

7. Eddie Stanky—Out of major league baseball since 1968 (he was coaching the University of South Alabama team), Stanky was invited to manage the Texas Rangers midway in the 1977 season. He managed two games, both victories, then quit. "I went back to my hotel room after the game," Stanky explained, "and laying in bed, I suddenly realized I didn't want to spend any more days on the road, away from home."

8. George Sauer Jr.—A star of the New York Jets' Super Bowl champions in 1969 and one of the best wide receivers in professional football, Sauer suddenly quit the game at the peak of his career, one year after he had caught eight passes for 133 yards in the Jets' 16-7 Super Bowl upset of the Baltimore Colts. His intention was to write a novel, which still has not been published.

9. Billy Martin—After winning two consecutive American League pennants in his first two full seasons as manager of the New York Yankees, Martin was under constant fire in his third year. Controversy surrounded him and the team was going badly. The last straw came when Martin made some uncomplimentary remarks about Yankee owner George Steinbrenner. On July 24, 1978, in Kansas City, Martin called a hasty press conference and tearfully announced he had "resigned" as manager of the Yankees, "the only job I ever wanted." Clearly, his "resignation" was not completely voluntary. But five days later, during ceremonies at their annual Old Timers Day, the Yankees dramatically announced that Martin would "unresign" and rejoin the Yankees as manager for the 1980 season.

10. Turkey Mike Donlin—Few athletes had as checkered a career as Donlin, an outfielder with several major league teams. In 1904, he was suspended by the New York Giants. He missed most of 1906 with a broken

leg. He held out the entire 1907 season in a contract dispute. He went on the voluntary retired list in the 1909 and 1910 seasons. And he finally quit for good in 1914 to go on the stage.

11. Dave Cowens—Bored and tired of the pro basketball grind, Cowens quit the Boston Celtics in the middle of the 1976–77 season, just one year after leading the Celtics to the NBA title. All sorts of rumors and speculation centered around Cowens' walkout—that he had an incurable illness, that he had a mental breakdown—and there were even reports that he had taken a job driving a taxi in Boston. Cowens merely explained he had "lost my enthusiasm for the game." He sat out 29 games, then returned because "it was harder for me not to play than to play."

12. Johnny Keane—With the St. Louis Cardinals trailing badly in the National League pennant race in August, 1964, the club refused to confirm that manager Keane would be back the following year. They let him suffer, while encouraging speculation of his dismissal. Finally, the Cardinals rallied to overtake the leaders and win the pennant on the final day of the season. Keane was the toast of St. Louis, a hero. The club owner, Gussie Busch, came to him, hat in hand, to ask him to return for the 1965 season. Keane told him what he could do with his job and resigned. The following season he was managing the New York Yankees.

13. Edd Roush—Unable to come to terms with the New York Giants (their difference was a mere $7,000), Roush refused to compromise his principles and sat out the entire 1930 season. The previous year, he had batted .324. The dispute was never resolved and Roush was traded to Cincinnati and finished out his career there.

14. Joe Namath—The toast of New York after leading the Jets to an upset victory in Super Bowl III, Namath an-

nounced his retirement two years later in a tear-filled press conference. He had been asked by NFL Commissioner Pete Rozelle to sell his interest in Bachelors III, a New York night spot of questionable repute, and Joe refused. Several weeks later, he relented, sold his piece of the club, and returned to quarterback the Jets.

15. Carl Mays—A mainstay of the Boston Red Sox' pitching staff, Mays had won 62 games from 1916 through 1918. In the following year, he got off to a bad start and was 5–11 in July. Somewhat paranoid, Mays suspected his teammates of deliberately letting him down, and on July 13, he jumped the team, saying, "Tell Ed Barrow [Boston manager] I've gone fishing. I'll never pitch another game for the Red Sox." Mays was right. He was sold to the Yankees for $40,000 and two players, and two years later led the league with 27 victories.

16. Adolf Hitler—His myth of Aryan supremacy destroyed by a 22-year-old American black named Jesse Owens, Hitler walked out of the Olympic stadium (supposedly to avoid a light rain) after Owens won his first of four gold medals in the 1936 Olympics in Berlin.

Adolf Hitler's walkout on Jesse Owens created endless controversy.

UPI

About the Authors

PHIL PEPE writes a column and covers the Yankees for the New York *Daily News*, and is the Yankee correspondent for *The Sporting News*. He has written a dozen books, including *From Ghetto to Glory: The Bob Gibson Story*, *The Wit and Wisdom of Yogi Berra: Winners Never Quit*, *Come Out Smokin': The Champ Nobody Knew*, and *Willis Reed's View from the Rim*.

ZANDER HOLLANDER, a former sportswriter on the *New York World-Telegram & Sun*, is president of Associated Features Inc., specialists in sports and recreational publishing. Among his book credits are *The Pro Basketball Encyclopedia*, *The Complete Encyclopedia of Ice Hockey* (with Hal Bock), *Madison Square Garden*, and *The Encyclopedia of Sports Talk*.